Blackboard® For Dummies

Cheat Sheet

The Blackboard Course Control Panel

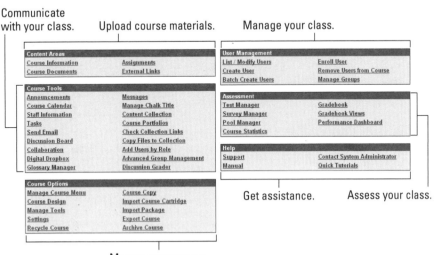

Communicate with your class.

Upload course materials.

Manage your class.

Get assistance.

Assess your class.

Manage your course.

- ✔ Upload your course materials and files by clicking a link in the Content Areas pane. This pane is most useful for getting the right stuff in front of your learners — and doing it fast (see Chapter 5).

- ✔ Use the features in the Course Tools pane to keep in touch with your learners and to allow them to keep in touch with you. Use this area also to manage the various tools available in Blackboard (see Chapter 6).

  Your institution may have some Blackboard features turned off or customized, so this picture might differ slightly from your own Control Panel. It should be close, though.

- ✔ Administer your course before it begins by changing the course menu, and after it ends by using the links in the Course Options pane to copy content to another course (see Chapters 4 and 10).

- ✔ Give learners access to your course, remove them or put them in groups, and perform other useful tasks from the User Management pane (see Chapter 3).

- ✔ Behold the power of the Assessment pane. From there, you test learners, survey them, grade them, and track their overall progress (see Chapter 8).

- ✔ Get help quickly by using the links inside the Help pane (see Chapter 15).

For Dummies: Bestselling Book Series for Beginners

Blackboard® For Dummies®

Cheat Sheet

The Text Box Editor

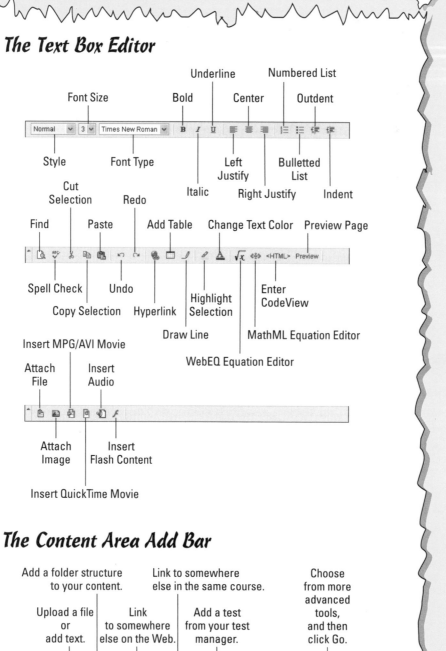

Font Size

Underline

Numbered List

Bold

Center

Outdent

Style

Font Type

Left Justify

Bulletted List

Italic

Right Justify

Indent

Cut Selection

Redo

Find

Paste

Add Table

Change Text Color

Preview Page

Spell Check

Undo

Enter CodeView

Copy Selection

Hyperlink

Highlight Selection

MathML Equation Editor

Draw Line

WebEQ Equation Editor

Insert MPG/AVI Movie

Attach File

Insert Audio

Attach Image

Insert Flash Content

Insert QuickTime Movie

The Content Area Add Bar

Add a folder structure to your content.

Link to somewhere else in the same course.

Choose from more advanced tools, and then click Go.

Upload a file or add text.

Link to somewhere else on the Web.

Add a test from your test manager.

For Dummies: Bestselling Book Series for Beginners

Blackboard®
FOR
DUMMIES®

Blackboard®
FOR
DUMMIES®

by Howie Southworth, Kemal Cakici,
Yianna Vovides, Susan Zvacek

Wiley Publishing, Inc.

Blackboard® For Dummies®

Published by
Wiley Publishing, Inc.
111 River Street
Hoboken, NJ 07030-5774
www.wiley.com

Copyright © 2006 by Wiley Publishing, Inc., Indianapolis, Indiana

Published by Wiley Publishing, Inc., Indianapolis, Indiana

Published simultaneously in Canada

For general information on our other products and services, please contact our Customer Care Department within the U.S. at 800-762-2974, outside the U.S. at 317-572-3993, or fax 317-572-4002.

For technical support, please visit www.wiley.com/techsupport.

Wiley also publishes its books in a variety of electronic formats. Some content that appears in print may not be available in electronic books.

Library of Congress Control Number: 2006920627

ISBN-13: 978-0-471-79832-3

ISBN-10: 0-471-79832-0

Manufactured in the United States of America

10 9 8 7 6 5 4 3

1O/RS/QU/QW/IN

WILEY

About the Authors

Howie Southworth is an experienced teacher, trainer, and facilitator with a background in both student and instructor development. His academic degrees are in computer science (BA) and higher education administration (MA). He has been consulting on the use of online course management systems for the past 5 years, and teaching people how to teach for the past 15. Howie has been invited to teach across the United States, Asia, and Europe. He is the director of education for the Disaster Recovery Institute International in Washington, D.C.

Yianna Vovides holds a PhD in instructional design and technology and works at The George Washington University, Washington, D.C. Dr. Vovides assists faculty with the integration of instructional technologies in teaching and learning. She is the lead instructor in the use of the Blackboard Learning System and Blackboard Content System and designs and implements learning environments for both blended-hybrid and fully online courses.

Kemal Cakici has expertise in designing and implementing information systems solutions in the contexts of education and healthcare and has worked as a consultant in industry. He has taught business, information systems, and engineering courses as a faculty member. His academic degrees are in mechanical engineering (BS and MS). He is completing his doctoral studies in information and decision systems focusing on predicting the acceptance and usage of Web-based information systems. Kemal is working as a senior consultant for IMS Government Solutions.

Susan M. Zvacek, director of instructional development and support at the University of Kansas, has been involved with educational technology for more than 20 years and has worked in community college, university, and corporate training environments. Dr. Zvacek's teaching experience includes faculty and dissertation advisor positions at the University of Northern Colorado, Old Dominion University, and Nova Southeastern University.

Authors' Acknowledgments

Susan Zvacek wishes to acknowledge the support, patience, and good humor of her husband, Tony Miller, along with her exemplary staff in instructional development and support at the University of Kansas.

Kemal Cakici wishes to acknowledge the endless friendships of his co-authors Yianna Vovides and Howie Southworth and the long-distance moral support of his mother, Zehra Cakici, and his brother, Husam Cakici.

Yianna Vovides wishes to acknowledge her family and her colleagues at The George Washington University's Instructional Technology Lab. Go, gang!

Howie Southworth wishes to acknowledge his family — Floridian, Nor'easter, and Canine included. He would especially like to thank his wife, Jessica Finnefrock, for supporting the work of a few real Dummies!

All the authors also want to thank one another for a balanced amount of hard work and lots of laughs! To reflect this appreciation, the order of authorship was randomly assigned (or we were too tired to remember the alphabet). Together, we also want to thank the Blackboard, Inc., family for all their support. One example is their gracious permission to use a sample Oceanography course that they put together for software documentation. We simply could not have had this opportunity without them!

Publisher's Acknowledgments

We're proud of this book; please send us your comments through our online registration form located at www.dummies.com/register/.

Some of the people who helped bring this book to market include the following:

Acquisitions, Editorial, and Media Development

Project Editor: Rebecca Whitney

Acquisitions Editor: Greg Croy

Technical Editor: Tracy Sokol Farley

Editorial Manager: Jodi Jensen

Media Development Specialists: Angela Denny, Kate Jenkins, Steven Kudirka, Kit Malone, Travis Silvers

Media Development Coordinator: Laura Atkinson

Media Project Supervisor: Laura Moss

Media Development Manager: Laura VanWinkle

Media Development Associate Producer: Richard Graves

Editorial Assistant: Amanda Foxworth

Cartoons: Rich Tennant (www.the5thwave.com)

Composition Services

Project Coordinator: Erin Smith

Layout and Graphics: Carl Byers, Andrea Dahl, Barbara Moore

Proofreaders: Leeann Harney, Christine Pingleton, Techbooks

Indexer: Techbooks

Publishing and Editorial for Technology Dummies

    Richard Swadley, Vice President and Executive Group Publisher

    Andy Cummings, Vice President and Publisher

    Mary Bednarek, Executive Acquisitions Director

    Mary C. Corder, Editorial Director

Publishing for Consumer Dummies

    Diane Graves Steele, Vice President and Publisher

    Joyce Pepple, Acquisitions Director

Composition Services

    Gerry Fahey, Vice President of Production Services

    Debbie Stailey, Director of Composition Services

Contents at a Glance

Table of Contents

. . . .

Introduction

• •

*O*n your way to class with another three-foot stack of handouts to dole out? Just told to add a 16th office hour to your already hectic calendar? Wrist cramping from grading all those exams? The Blackboard Learning System can help you out! This rich, online course-management system provides you, the instructor, with the tools to easily present class materials on the Web, communicate online with an entire class, and track what the heck they're learning in there — from the comfort of your laptop, if that's where you're working. *Blackboard For Dummies* is a kinder, gentler way to learn how to use Blackboard as an instructor. This book isn't designed to be read from cover to cover (we won't tell anyone if you really want to, though) — it's the handy desk reference you've been looking for. Feel free to skip right to the essentials!

Who Should Buy This Book?

The real answer to this question is *everyone*. This book has terrific characters and edge-of-your-seat suspense, and it's a real page-turner. The yellow-and-black motif goes superbly with your collection of bumblebees. Okay, seriously, whether you're teaching a fully online course, a hybrid course (part classroom, part online), or a fully live course (with online dreams), *Blackboard For Dummies* provides you with the necessary tools of the trade.

Those who have access to teaching with Blackboard probably already know it. Typically, your school's, university's, or organization's contract with Blackboard, Inc., gives you the access you need. The following list describes the types of Blackboard licenses you might have within your reach:

✔ The **Blackboard Learning System** is otherwise known as the *Enterprise* edition (although it has nothing to do with Captain Kirk). The system allows for the complete integration of Blackboard software with other collections of information and data within your place of business, such as an enrollment or course registration system. This edition can also be expanded with many third-party software applications, called Building Blocks (see Chapter 4). Everything covered in this book can be used in the Enterprise edition.

✔ The Blackboard Learning System **Basic Edition** is the lightweight counterpart to the *Enterprise* edition we just mentioned. (It's normally a bit cheaper too.) You can do 98 percent of what's in this book. What doesn't exist in Basic Edition is some Adaptive Release of Content (see Chapter 5) and internal Blackboard messages (see Chapter 6). Basic Edition doesn't tie in to other sources of student information within your institution and has limited ability with Building Blocks.

✔ The Blackboard Learning System via **Course Sites** is one of those little-known value buys of the universe. Did you know that any industrious instructor, teacher, or trainer with access to the Internet and a few hundred bucks can develop, completely on her own, a fully loaded course using the Blackboard Learning System? Course Sites is a one-at-a-time, fee-based product to get adventurous teachers using Blackboard on their own (see Appendix D).

Foolish Assumptions

In grade school you might have learned the consequences of making assumptions. In the following list of assumptions we make about you, we brave those waters and throw caution to the wind. Although *Blackboard For Dummies* is a kinder and gentler reference guide, we have to let you know where we draw the line:

✔ **You know how to access the Internet from your home and from work.** That might sound simplistic, but we have to make sure that you're reading the right Dummies book. Blackboard is an online program, and online you must be.

✔ **You know that when we refer to *Blackboard,* we're not talking about the dusty, chalky, please-don't-scrape-your-fingernails-against-it thing.** We don't really like dust, that scraping noise drives us mad, and a couple of us have bad memories of having to stay after school to sponge down that darned chalkboard. Having said that, just let us write about online education — a lot — and we'll be okay.

✔ **You know where to find files on your computer.** We don't talk much about the Windows or Macintosh operating systems, and we don't preach about the good things that come along with healthy folder organization (well, maybe just a little). You should locate your files and course materials before going into this whole Blackboard world. Seriously.

✔ **Your institution or organization has access to the Blackboard Learning System, or you have access through Blackboard Course Sites.** This book wouldn't be a good buy just for great bedtime reading. It might produce the best dreams ever, but, seriously, you should go to sleep reading about dream-type subjects.

✔ **You're responsible for putting together a course, a training workshop, or something close to education.** We're all about helping you in the heat of the moment while you're pulling together materials, setting up your environment, and communicating with those about to learn something from you. If you're not teaching until next semester and won't be developing your course until a month from now, we're still happy to see you buy this book. Just don't forget where you put it. (Maybe that's why it's the color of sunrays.)

✔ **Depending on how Blackboard is laid out or managed at your institution, you might or might not have access to a feature or two that we describe in this book.** Some institutions take on administrative tasks themselves and don't need instructors to enroll their own learners in their courses, for example. We wrote this book on the assumption that all features are turned on. If you start to try something out and notice that it doesn't work, simply go to your Blackboard system administrator (your best friend) and find out what else might be turned off.

What's in This Book?

Blackboard For Dummies attempts to make the Blackboard Learning System easy to understand and use for all instructors, everywhere. It's written to keep the average user from pulling out what's left of his hair, the mid-level user from forgetting where everything is, and the advanced user from losing interest as she starts using the newest version of the program. We won't go too deep, and we promise that it won't hurt a bit.

Part I: What's Blackboard All About?

Quick — call the course-creation squad! Ah, it's the stuff of dreams. Assuming that you're building a course on your own and (like most of the civilized world) might not have lots of time on your hands, you need one or two things: a guide to get you moving quickly and perhaps a suggested path to complete course development for the Web. The first part of this book hands over these two solutions on a silver platter and gets you going in a meaningful (and heartfelt) way. You'll walk into Part I with a vision and walk out with the start of a beautiful product.

Part II: Easing into Blackboard

Ever wonder how all those news articles, wedding albums, and random garage-fare on eBay find their way onto the Internet? You're about to find out. This part of the book focuses on how to get your stuff organized, uploaded, and beamed out to the screens of your audience without reinventing the wheel. We start out nice and easy with the topic of getting learners online and rarin' to go. We continue with the nuts and bolts of uploading course materials. Then, we round out everything with a stirring rendition about how to communicate with your class through Blackboard.

Part III: Earning Your Blackboard Black Belt

You've done well, young grasshopper. You have grabbed the fly with your chopsticks and will now be quickly be transformed into a Blackboard Master. This part of the book takes you beyond the program's simple features and empowers you to leverage Blackboard to improve learning. It's *huge.* You'll also figure out how to give out a quiz that you don't have to grade by hand. After presenting a virtual laundry list of additional tools, we'll show you the magic that is online grading and demonstrate how to reuse the same course over and over again. To quizzes . . . and beyond!

Part IV: The Part of Tens

This traditional part of a *For Dummies* book is chock-full of additional tips from the twisted brains of the authors. This part extols the virtues of a well-tuned course menu, the true value of good organization (don't stop reading just because of that one), the best questions to ask your system administrator, and the "vroom vroom" effect of good online communication, among other tried-and-true ideas from the minds of genius.

Part V: Appendixes

The appendixes in the back of this book supplement your Blackboard experience by adding all kinds of useful information. You can read about teaching with the help of technology, get an overview of the Blackboard Content System, and fill out a handy checklist of items you might have forgotten or want to add later. We even give you a guide to handy resources on the Web so that you can continue to add to your information arsenal. Finally, the glossary clues you in to the meaning of all kinds of Blackboard terms.

Conventions Used in This Book

To get the maximum benefit from this book, you need to understand the terms and concepts we list in this section.

Whenever we point out something in the text that you see on your screen, we use a special font, `like this`. Whenever we want you to type something in a set of steps, we use a **boldface font**.

We write steps showing you how to use Blackboard features by using the Control Panel as a springboard. Everything we do starts there. In any chapter that has steps in it, we begin with a Tip paragraph that covers how to get back to the Control Panel if you get lost or get logged out of Blackboard. We place heavy emphasis on the Control Panel as your headquarters because you can simply do everything important from there. To save yourself one click, however, you can also use the Edit View for Content Areas option. Although Edit view allows you to skip the step of going to the Control Panel, to be honest, we believe that the Control Panel brings you, the instructor, a relaxed, at-home type of feeling.

When we refer to *learners* throughout this book, we mean students. "Why," you might ask, "are you using such a weird word to spell out a simple concept?" Within higher education, grades K–12, and sometimes in the training world, *student* means one thing; in corporate life, most training worlds, and certification realms, however, many people prefer to go by some other word: trainee, test-taker, team member, or perhaps "mentee." We have found that the generic term *learner* meets with approval from most people because, after all, what's going on (you hope) inside this application? Learning.

We refer to your *Blackboard system administrator* as your "best friend" many times in this book. We realize that you might not have a Blackboard system administrator using that exact title, and that person might not truly be your best friend, if he or she even exists. You do, however, have support when using Blackboard. You might receive that support from the help desk staff, the teaching and learning center, the supersmart techie down the hall, or even Blackboard, Inc., when it provides you with direct support for Course Sites.

The *cursor,* or *pointer,* is the arrow that moves around the screen as you move your mouse around the mouse pad. The cursor might also refer to the I-beam that appears in the text in such a way that when you click and drag along a line of text, you highlight (or *select*) the text. A *drop-down menu* is the part of a Blackboard form that's used to select from a list of choices, such as when you choose a question type to add to a Blackboard test. When you click one of those menus, a list descends from the top and you see your choices. Although it all makes sense when you begin to use the program, we wanted to give you a head's-up about these terms.

Clicking means pressing, just once, the leftmost button on top of your mouse and releasing it. In case you're using a Macintosh single-button mouse, leftmost still means leftmost, which in the case of a single button is also the rightmost button. Don't get confused. When we refer to clicking something, it usually means pointing the cursor to and activating a button, menu, or link on the screen. *Double-clicking* means clicking twice in rapid succession. You usually do this when you're selecting a file in a folder in Windows or in the Macintosh operating system.

Icons Used in This Book

Above and beyond our step-by-step instructions for using Blackboard lies a set of great ideas from your dutiful authors. We look at these tips like icing on the cake. (When was the last time you scraped icing off your cake?) We think that they're wonderful.

Like the Tip icon, the Remember icon points you toward key ingredients to using Blackboard in a smart way. These paragraphs mostly point out things we think you should always keep in mind.

If we think that you might mess something up, we warn you. Trust us. We trust you quite a bit, mostly because you're reading, or considering reading, this book, so we throw in only a scant few warnings for good measure throughout the text. Frankly, a few tasks within Blackboard qualify as tricky, and we want only the best for your experience.

This icon doesn't appear much, and it's not for the weak of heart. Are you scared yet? The technical stuff we talk about usually refers to something outside of Blackboard that might affect the way things work inside Blackboard. One example is the types of files you might want to upload, and another is the way Blackboard handles filenames differently on PCs and Macs.

You're not alone in the universe. Blackboard is being used in higher education, in K–12 education, in the military, in corporate life, and on Mars, with the unfortunate but suspicious exception of that last one. In addition to getting tips from your lovely yet rugged authors, throughout this book you can find ideas contributed by instructors, teachers, and trainers from around the globe. You might even read the wisdom of an instructor just like you. How's that for service?

Where to Go from Here

We know that you're chomping at the bit to start using Blackboard. After getting information from your institution about how to access your Blackboard Web site (just ask someone there to tell you the Internet address), flip on your Internet-connected computer and prepare to wow your colleagues, awe your friends, impress your family, and take your learners to the next level. Part I has your quick-start guide, and you'll know quickly if that's where you're comfortable starting out. Good luck and blast off!

Part I
What's Blackboard All About?

"As a Web site designer, I never thought I'd say this, but I don't think your site has enough bells and whistles."

In this part . . .

This part of the book is only the beginning of something wonderful for both you and your learners. Trust us, and we'll make your life easy (at least the online part of your academic life!). The inaugural part of *Blackboard For Dummies* starts you off nice and easy with a first-timer's look at the real deal and finishes off with a loud round of applause from you, the reader. We'll take you to a place where you're the superorganized instructor, prepared to delve into the very heart of every Blackboard use.

Chapter 1 hands to you a brief overview of what you see on the inside of Blackboard. Call it a geography course that presents a visual guide through the elements on your Blackboard screen that you'll want to know about before diving in. What does your Control Panel look like? What are bread crumbs, anyhow? Look forward to answers to these questions and many more.

Chapter 2 begins with a quick-start guide to using Blackboard at a minimum, from uploading a syllabus file to entering grades into the Gradebook. The chapter concludes by giving you a methodical path to walk that includes all the grand details of planning a comprehensive Blackboard course, from soup to nuts.

Let's get this party started!

Chapter 1

Your First Look at Blackboard

In This Chapter

▶ Introducing Blackboard

▶ Finding your way in the course

▶ Mapping out the Control Panel

▶ Discovering a few shortcuts

*W*e understand that finding how to use a new application or even staying up-to-date with upgrades and new features can be overwhelming, especially with Web-based applications. You may ask, "Why is that?" The reason is that, depending on which browser you use, you may or may not encounter problems for some items versus others, and some features are supported in one browser and not in another. The list of issues can seem endless at times.

You may also be wondering why we're starting out this chapter with a less-than-motivational introduction. The reason is that what you will love about Blackboard may also be the source of some frustration, much like in other Web-based applications you may be using. Remember that you're working on the Web, and keep in mind the four concepts in the following list. (The first letter of each concept combines to create, sort of, the acronym *AKA Bb* — or "also known as Blackboard" — so we use that as a mnemonic device to help you remember.) Here's our list:

✔ **A**ccess — get connected: To access Blackboard, you need to have Internet access. That's the beauty of Web-based applications such as Blackboard: After you get connected to the Internet, you can access your Blackboard account from any Internet-connected computer anywhere.

✔ **K**nowledge — know your browser: Get comfortable with the options in your browser, such as enlarging or reducing text size, locating or setting your default folder for downloading files, and enabling or disabling your pop-up blocker. Allowing pop-ups is important because Blackboard utilizes pop-ups for some of its functions.

    ✔ **A**ddress — remember your Blackboard URL: You probably know many ways to access your Blackboard login page and have already book-marked all of them, right? Just in case your memory fails you, write down your Blackboard Web address and keep it in your back pocket so that you can access it from any Internet-connected computer anywhere. Also keep your institution's IT help desk number handy, just in case you have no idea what the address is.

    ✔ **B**e aware and **b**eware. Make yourself aware of the instructional tools that Blackboard offers, and keep in mind that you should test your course environment thoroughly before releasing it to your learners.

If you haven't taught online, be sure to consult the appendixes in this book for some additional support in using Blackboard effectively. Blackboard is designed to offer you much flexibility in your course design, so take advantage of it!

Logging In to Blackboard

Blackboard is a secure Web-based application that requires all its users to enter their unique login information (username and password) in order to access the courses they are either teaching or are enrolled in (see Figure 1-1). To be able to log in to Blackboard at your institution, find out what that login information is. Your Blackboard administrator or your institution's IT help desk should be able to provide you with this information. While you're at it, find out what the URL is for the Blackboard login page at your institution. You need to have these two key pieces of information at hand to get your first look at Blackboard.

Figure 1-1:
Logging
in to
Blackboard.

> **Login Here**
>
> Have an account? Enter login information here and click the Login button below.
>
> Username:
> [   ]
>
> Password:
> [   ]
>
> Forgot your password?   (Login)
>
> Download Blackboard Backpack

The Visual Text Box Editor (WYSIWYG) editor in Blackboard works only with Internet Explorer. Although Blackboard supports all major browsers for all other functionalities, the Visual Text Box Editor doesn't display all available functions if you use another browser to access Blackboard.

Navigating Your Way Around Blackboard

In every Blackboard course, you, the instructor, can customize the course menu to your liking and in effect allow or disallow navigation options for your learners. In other words, Blackboard allows you to include a course map as part of the menu. Because the *course map* is a navigational map, a user can jump to any item in the course. In addition, you can display the course menu in either Quick view or Detail view. When both views are enabled, therefore, a user can either expand the menu in Detail view (thus making it more like the course map) or use Quick view to click the menu items (buttons or text) to navigate to a desired area of the course (see Figure 1-2).

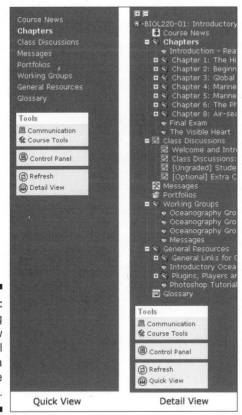

Figure 1-2: Comparing Quick view and Detail view on a course menu.

As you're building your Blackboard course, you should keep track of your bread crumb trail. No, we don't mean to insult your eating habits; we're referring to the trail of links at the top of the page in any Blackboard course. You may have noticed this type of link in other Web environments. The deeper you get into a course, the more the trail expands and the more easily you can navigate back to where you came from by using the bread crumb links (see Figure 1-3).

Figure 1-3:
The bread
crumb trail.

COURSES > -BIOL220-01: INTRODUCTORY OCEANOGRAPHY 01 > CHAPTERS > CHAPTER 1: THE HISTORY OF OCEAN EXPLORATION AND OCEAN SCIENCE

Get in the habit of using the bread crumbs as an orienting tool in the course while adding or modifying content items. After you develop this habit, which, by the way, is a good habit to have for any Web-based application, you don't make mistakes when you're adding folders and items and end up wasting your time. You can simply look up, check your bread crumb trail, and know whether you're in the correct location in the course before you start adding content.

Clicking the course title always takes you to the entry page of the course, which is basically to the view that learners have.

Traversing the course Control Panel

In your Blackboard course, you have access to the Control Panel — and your learners don't (see Figure 1-4). You therefore have the power to add, modify, copy, and remove content; turn course tools on or off; and decide how to display the Course Menu and in what language (or locale). With the power to manage the Control Panel comes great responsibility: to provide your learners with a well-designed learning environment.

Note that your first look at your Blackboard course is determined by what the powers that be at your institution decided to include on the Course Menu. With Control Panel access, however, you can customize your learners' first look at your Blackboard course. So, plan before you implement.

To help you plan, think of the course Control Panel as being composed of these areas:

- ✔ Course administration
- ✔ Course materials
- ✔ Communication and collaboration
- ✔ Assessment

Content Areas		User Management	
Course Information	Assignments	List / Modify Users	Enroll User
Course Documents	External Links	Create User	Remove Users from Course
		Batch Create Users	Manage Groups

Course Tools		Assessment	
Announcements	Messages	Test Manager	Gradebook
Course Calendar	Manage Chalk Title	Survey Manager	Gradebook Views
Staff Information	Content Collection	Pool Manager	Performance Dashboard
Tasks	Course Portfolios	Course Statistics	
Send Email	Check Collection Links		
Discussion Board	Copy Files to Collection	Help	
Collaboration	Add Users by Role	Support	Contact System Administrator
Digital Dropbox	Advanced Group Management	Manual	Quick Tutorials
Glossary Manager	Discussion Grader		

Course Options	
Manage Course Menu	Course Copy
Course Design	Import Course Cartridge
Manage Tools	Import Package
Settings	Export Course
Recycle Course	Archive Course

Figure 1-4: A first look at the course Control Panel.

Course administration

Your course administration options (see Figure 1-5) reside mostly in the Course Options pane. You can use these options to customize the course menu, enable or disable course tools, change the course availability and entry page, and import, copy, export, and archive your course. In addition to all these instructor administration options in your course, we have good news for language instructors and international readers: You can now customize your Blackboard course interface so that it's displayed in one of eight languages.

Course Options		User Management	
Manage Course Menu	Course Copy	List / Modify Users	Enroll User
Course Design	Import Course Cartridge	Create User	Remove Users from Course
Manage Tools	Import Package	Batch Create Users	Manage Groups
Settings	Export Course		
Recycle Course	Archive Course		

Figure 1-5: Course administration options.

If your institution or organization has the Blackboard Academic Suite or the Blackboard Learning System (but not the Basic Edition), you as an instructor can set the language of the course independently from the language setting of the overall system. Blackboard supports English, Spanish, French, Italian, German, Dutch, Portuguese, Japanese, and simplified Chinese (see Figure 1-6).

Depending on how your institution handles user accounts and course creation and modification, you may or may not be able to create and modify user accounts, create courses, and enroll or remove users from a course. These options are available in the User Management pane.

Course materials

Course materials — such as your syllabus, readings, assignments, and tests — can be added to the Content Areas of your course (see Figure 1-7).

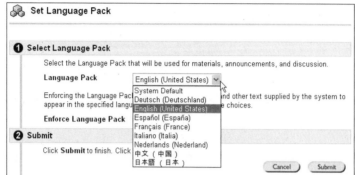

Figure 1-6:
Setting the language for a course.

Figure 1-7:
Managing the course materials.

In any Content Area, in fact, you can use these options to perform a task:

- ✔ **Item:** Create content and upload files.
- ✔ **Folder:** Layer or organize content.
- ✔ **Course Link:** Create links to other areas within the same course.
- ✔ **External Link:** Create links to an external Web site.
- ✔ **Test:** Add a test.
- ✔ **Learning Unit:** Develop a sequential set of items or a tutorial.
- ✔ **Survey:** Survey your learners or take a poll.
- ✔ **Assignment:** Add an assignment for paperless feedback and grading.
- ✔ **Offline Content:** Access offline content on a CD-ROM, for example.
- ✔ **Syllabus:** Create a new syllabus and lessons.

You can also perform these tasks in any Content Area:

- ✔ Import SCORM, IMS, or NLN content by using the desired content-packaging option.
- ✔ Select a tool option to link to individual tools, such as Discussion Boards, Chat, Virtual Classroom, Group, and more.

If your institution uses the Blackboard Learning System, Basic Edition, you cannot include SCORM objects.

Note that when you use these options to add content to your course, you can also manage the content item by enabling Adaptive Release of Content, accessing tracking, and reviewing status tracking (see Figure 1-8).

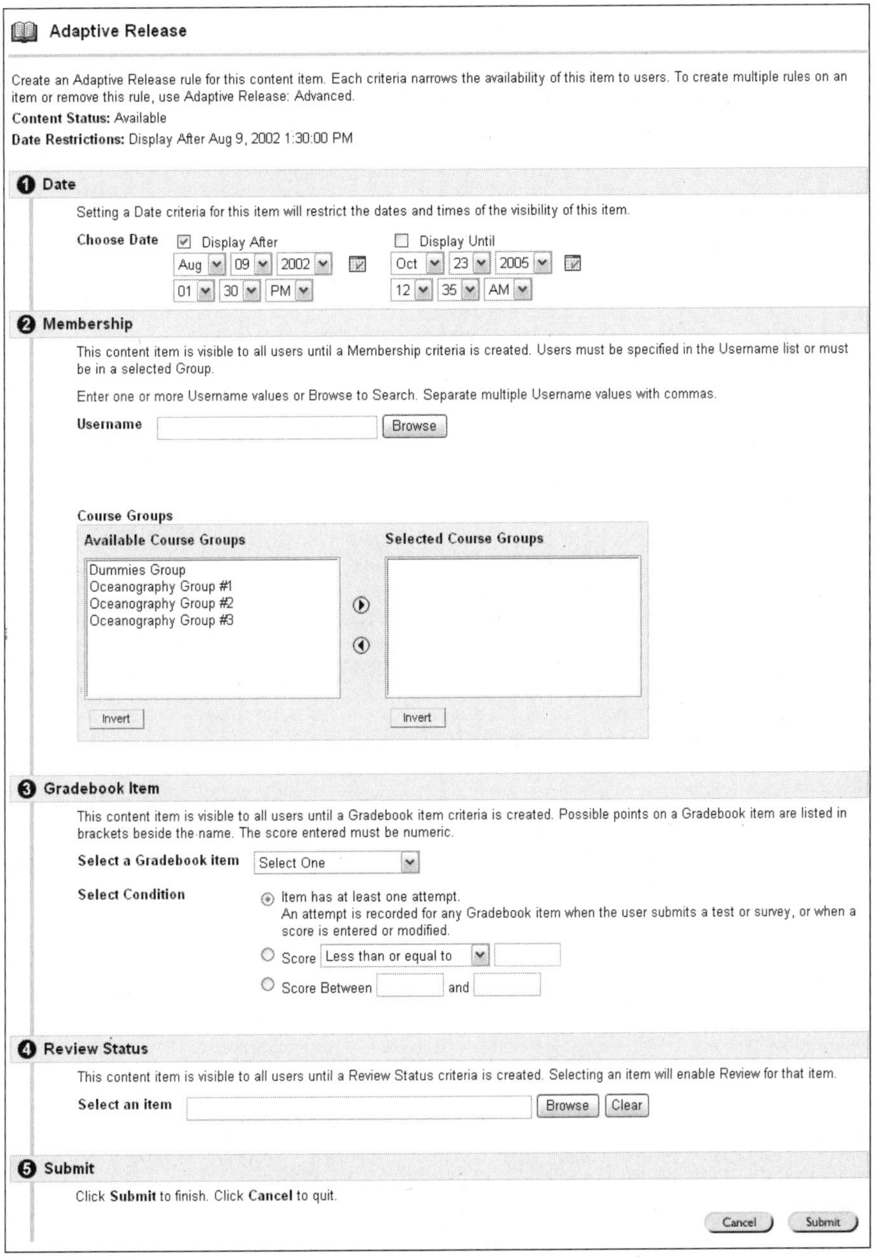

Adaptive Release

Create an Adaptive Release rule for this content item. Each criteria narrows the availability of this item to users. To create multiple rules on an item or remove this rule, use Adaptive Release: Advanced.
Content Status: Available
Date Restrictions: Display After Aug 9, 2002 1:30:00 PM

❶ Date

Setting a Date criteria for this item will restrict the dates and times of the visibility of this item.

Choose Date ☑ Display After   ☐ Display Until
Aug ▾ 09 ▾ 2002 ▾ 📅   Oct ▾ 23 ▾ 2005 ▾ 📅
01 ▾ 30 ▾ PM ▾   12 ▾ 35 ▾ AM ▾

❷ Membership

This content item is visible to all users until a Membership criteria is created. Users must be specified in the Username list or must be in a selected Group.

Enter one or more Username values or Browse to Search. Separate multiple Username values with commas.

Username [   ] [Browse]

Course Groups

Available Course Groups   **Selected Course Groups**
Dummies Group
Oceanography Group #1
Oceanography Group #2   ▶
Oceanography Group #3
                                       ◀

[Invert]   [Invert]

❸ Gradebook Item

This content item is visible to all users until a Gradebook item criteria is created. Possible points on a Gradebook item are listed in brackets beside the name. The score entered must be numeric.

Select a Gradebook item [Select One   ▾]

Select Condition ⦿ Item has at least one attempt.
An attempt is recorded for any Gradebook item when the user submits a test or survey, or when a score is entered or modified.
○ Score [Less than or equal to ▾] [   ]
○ Score Between [   ] and [   ]

❹ Review Status

This content item is visible to all users until a Review Status criteria is created. Selecting an item will enable Review for that item.
Select an item [   ] [Browse] [Clear]

❺ Submit

Click **Submit** to finish. Click **Cancel** to quit.
                                                    (Cancel) (Submit)

Figure 1-8:
An Adaptive
Release of
Content
item.

Additional options may be available to you as part of the Content Area interface, depending on whether your institution has added third-party products or building blocks within the Blackboard course environment.

Communication and collaboration tools

Communication tools — such as announcements, collaboration, e-mail, a discussion board, and messages — are available in your course Control Panel and can be included as links within Content Areas or as course links on the course menu (see Figure 1-9).

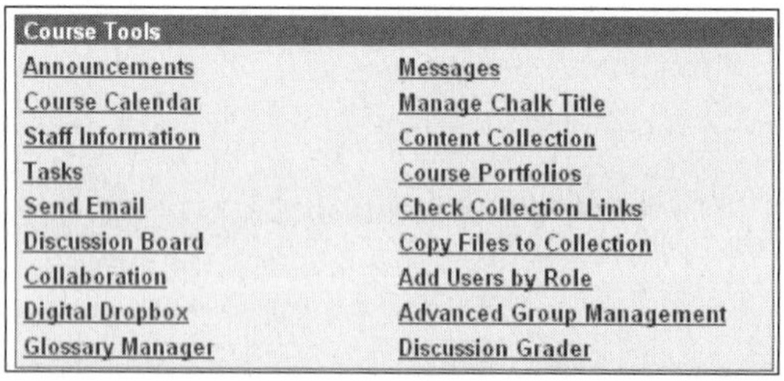

Figure 1-9:
Communication and collaboration tools.

Course Tools	
Announcements	Messages
Course Calendar	Manage Chalk Title
Staff Information	Content Collection
Tasks	Course Portfolios
Send Email	Check Collection Links
Discussion Board	Copy Files to Collection
Collaboration	Add Users by Role
Digital Dropbox	Advanced Group Management
Glossary Manager	Discussion Grader

Some of the tools available to you in the Course Tools pane are highlighted in Table 1-1. Again, depending on your institution's Blackboard setup, you may have access to more or fewer tools.

Table 1-1	Communication Tools in Blackboard	
Tool Name	*Purpose*	*Use Case*
Announcements	Inform users	Use this tool when you want to remind learners of assignment deadlines or upcoming events, for example. Don't use it when you want to communicate with immediacy, because learners must be logged in to Blackboard to view your announcements.
Staff Information	Post user profile	Use the Staff Information tool to post information about you, your teaching assistants (TAs), section leaders, and guest lecturers, for example, in the course. Don't use the Staff Information tool if your goal is to have your learners post their own, personal profiles; direct them to use the Student Homepage instead.

Tool Name	Purpose	Use Case
Course Calendar	Inform users	Use the Course Calendar to add descriptions of sessions or lessons and upcoming events, for example. Use the Course Calendar in conjunction with announcements to reinforce deadlines and help learners stay on track. Don't use the Course Calendar if you're going to keep it hidden in the Tools area of the course: Be sure to unbury it by creating course links from your menu or Content Areas, or both.
Tasks	Define and organize user activities	Use the Tasks tool to provide learners with a list of activities with set due dates while allowing them to monitor the list of activities and prioritize those tasks. As with many of the course tools, don't use Tasks if you're not planning to integrate it into your course design and track learners' progress status regularly.
Send Email	Inform users	Use the Send Email tool when you want to let learners know of a change in class location or a cancellation or change in an exam or assignment due date. Use Send Email in conjunction with the Announcements tool to reinforce your message. Don't use Send Email in Blackboard to generate class discussions because it doesn't act like a distribution list: To the people receiving the mail, it looks as though they're the only ones receiving it.
Discussion Board	Carry out group discussion asynchronously	Use the Discussion Board tool to have learners post discussion questions, respond to each other, lead discussions, engage in peer review, and more. With a bit of creativity, you will find that the discussion board has a myriad of uses. Don't use it if you want to engage in real-time discussion; use the collaboration tools instead.

(continued)

Table 1-1 *(continued)*

Tool Name	Purpose	Use Case
Collaboration	Carry out group discussion synchronously	Use the Chat or Virtual Classroom options in the Collaboration tool to hold virtual office hours and to replace or supplement face-to-face class time, for example. Don't use Chat or Virtual Classroom with large groups unless you're a whiz! Having more than a handful of folks in a Collaboration room can get chaotic, if you don't manage it well.

Assessment tools

The Assessment options available to you in Blackboard are extensive and flexible, with more than 15 different question types for creating tests, surveys, and question pools. In addition, you can upload your own questions all at one time and select questions from existing assessments or pools in your course.

The Gradebook allows you to use weights for your assessment items; display grades in score, letter, percentage, or text entry; or create your own customized display of the grade. You can modify the range of scores within the Gradebook settings so that it conforms to your own course-grading criteria for displaying letter grades. You can download the Gradebook, modify it in a spreadsheet program, such as Excel, and upload it back into Blackboard. Your learners can then view their individual grades by using their My Grades tool.

We have to mention a couple more things about the Assessment options in your Blackboard course: the Performance Dashboard (see Figure 1-10) and Course Statistics (see Figure 1-11). The Performance Dashboard allows you to view an individual user's access of content utilizing adaptive release and/or review.

The Course Statistics screen offers you a summary of access data for overall or specific tools and pages in the course.

Had enough? We could go on and on about the Assessment options in Blackboard, but we do that elsewhere in this book.

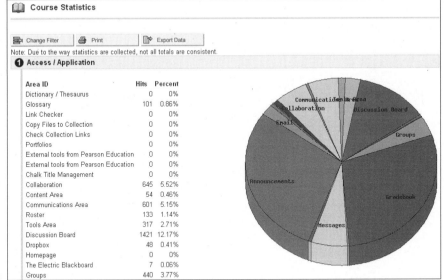

Figure 1-10: A view of the Performance Dashboard.

Performance Dashboard

Use the links provided to view user progress details for each performance measurement.

🖨 Print

Last Name	First Name	Username	Role	Last Login	Days Since Last Login	Review Status	Adaptive Release	View Grades
Demo	AS	asdemo	Instructor	Jan 19, 2006 11:27:04 AM	0	0	🔘	
Chu	Cathy	cchu	Instructor	Jan 19, 2006 9:30:38 AM	0	36	🔘	
Cruz	Cindy	ccruz	Student	Dec 2, 2005 2:32:50 PM	47	2	🔘	▤
Randall	Caroline	crandall	Instructor	Jun 23, 2005 6:40:58 PM	209	0	🔘	
Goldman	Greg	ggoldman	Student	Oct 12, 2004 5:28:38 PM	463	0	🔘	▤
Holland	Hector	hholland	Student	Nov 13, 2005 10:58:07 PM	66	0	🔘	▤
Foster	Jessica	jfoster	Instructor	Jan 10, 2006 12:00:32 PM	8	0	🔘	
Foster	Jess	jfosters	Student	Dec 22, 2005 11:34:21 AM	28	0	🔘	▤
Foster	Jessie	jfostert	Instructor	Nov 9, 2005 4:32:25 PM	70	0	🔘	
Jones	Jeremy	jjones	Student	Dec 28, 2005 3:30:45 PM	21	0	🔘	▤
Smith	John	jsmith	Student	Never	Never	0	🔘	▤

Figure 1-11: A simple view of Course Statistics.

Course Statistics

📋 Change Filter   🖨 Print   📑 Export Data

Note: Due to the way statistics are collected, not all totals are consistent.

❶ Access / Application

Area ID	Hits	Percent
Dictionary / Thesaurus	0	0%
Glossary	101	0.86%
Link Checker	0	0%
Copy Files to Collection	0	0%
Check Collection Links	0	0%
Portfolios	0	0%
External tools from Pearson Education	0	0%
External tools from Pearson Education	0	0%
Chalk Title Management	0	0%
Collaboration	645	5.52%
Content Area	54	0.46%
Communications Area	601	5.15%
Roster	133	1.14%
Tools Area	317	2.71%
Discussion Board	1421	12.17%
Dropbox	48	0.41%
Homepage	0	0%
The Electric Blackboard	7	0.06%
Groups	440	3.77%

Comparing Edit view and Display view

As we mention earlier in this chapter, in the section "Traversing the course Control Panel," the Control Panel offers you the ability to take control of your Web-based course environment, much like, if you please, a captain at the helm of a ship. It's not like you're steering the *Titanic,* but rather like guiding Darwin's *Beagle,* or Columbus's *Nina, Pinta,* and *Santa Maria.*

To make adding and editing your content in the Content Areas more flexible, Blackboard also offers you two views of your course: Edit and Display. Think of these views as shortcuts into and out of the Control Panel (much like a wormhole — too much, right?). As you navigate in your course by using the Course Menu, as though you were a learner in the course, notice in the Content Areas the Edit View link, to the right of the bread crumb trail, in the upper-right area of the screen.

Clicking the Edit View link, in the upper-right corner of the screen, enables you to edit the content items you have in the Content Area you're in without having to access that area by clicking the Control Panel link and then clicking the Content Area's name from the Content Areas pane. After you're in Edit view (see Figure 1-12), you can add new content and modify, remove, manage, copy, and move existing content items by using the tools available to you in the Content Area.

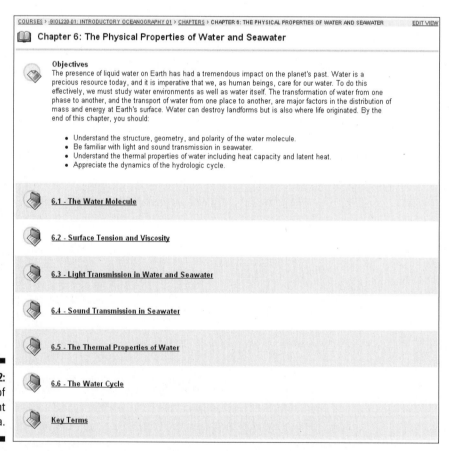

Figure 1-12: Edit view of a Content Area.

Note that after you're in Edit view, the link name changes to Display View. Clicking the Display View link allows you to view the Content Area without all the editing and tool options displayed. After you're back in Display view (see Figure 1-13), you again navigate your Blackboard course much like the rest of the passengers onboard the ship (okay, fine — much like your learners in the course).

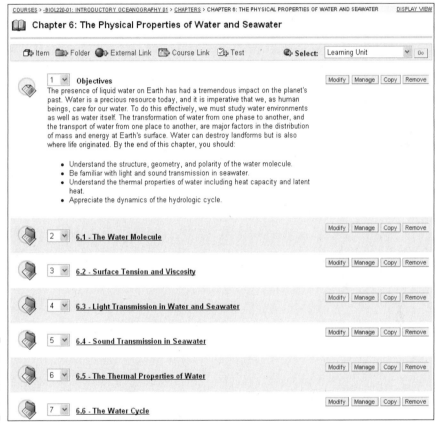

Figure 1-13: Display view of a Content Area.

Chapter 2

The Course-Development Process

*T*his chapter provides you with the necessary tools to get the course ball rolling in an efficient and smart way. If you're the type of person who thinks in a mystery-novel-like manner, you probably already read Chapter 1 and got yourself comfortable with the new scenery. Now that you know the lay of Blackboard Land, you're at the next natural step: Put it to good use.

Because of a heavy process focus within course development, this chapter (and only this chapter!) veers away from the standard *Dummies* reference concept a little and assumes that you're reading the chapter mostly in order. This statement is especially true of the quick-start guide in the first half of this chapter. In the second half of this chapter, we describe the most important ways (and Blackboard has a ton of them) that you can customize your course to fit your instructional needs. Believe it or not, putting these two halves together yourself sets you apart from the average instructor!

After you're familiar with the ton of ways in which you can engage quick and methodical course development within Blackboard, you definitely will want to explore some features in greater detail. Look in Parts II and III for detailed, step-by-step instructions and time-tested ideas for using Blackboard effectively.

For more detailed information about these processes and much more, check out the Table of Contents to find chapters containing extensive instructions for each Blackboard feature, tips and tricks for performing all kinds of tasks, and suggestions for integrating Blackboard functionality into your course to enhance both teaching and learning.

For all of the features described in this chapter, you should start at your course Control Panel. We like to call it "home base" when no one else is around. Follow these steps to get where you need to be:

1. **Log in to Blackboard using your username and password.**

   Assuming that your Web browser is open and you navigated your way to your institution's Blackboard start page, this step shouldn't be a problem. If it is, refer to Chapter 1 and remind yourself about your first time navigating through Blackboard. (Ah, memories.)

2. **On your Course List page, click the name of your course.**

   Your course name is a hyperlink, in blue text and underlined. This step also helps you see the way your learners will experience your course.

3. **Click the Control Panel link.**

   Locate this link at the bottom of the course menu, on the left side of your screen. Your gut should tell you to click this link every time you want to do something important in your Blackboard course.

A Quick-Start Guide: Get on the Fast Track with the Fab Four

As we promise in the introduction to this chapter, we dive in head-first, by helping you work through our own personal Fab Four:

- ✔ Post your syllabus.
- ✔ Give online assignments.
- ✔ Set up your Gradebook.
- ✔ Start online discussions.

This section does exactly what it promises: It gets you going *quickly*. We skip over many of the details and get right to the most popular functions within Blackboard.

Because this section is simply a quick-start guide, we have to assume some basic information about you. If our assumptions aren't correct, check out the areas we specify and then come back to this section to get started. We assume that you

- ✔ Have a Blackboard account (refer to Chapter 1 if you don't).
- ✔ Know how to get to your Blackboard page on the Web (again, refer to Chapter 1).

✔ Have at least one course already on your list (see the section "Starting a Brand-New Course," later in this chapter).

Tracy Russo, assistant professor of communication studies at the University of Kansas, says, "If you and your students are new to Blackboard, don't try to use all the features at once. It's better for instructors and students to start with just a few elements and learn how they work for the particular topic and class. It can be tonic for a class to incorporate other elements later in the semester."

Post your syllabus

First, you have to post your course syllabus. How else can your audience know that you give 10 bonus points just for showing up? Follow these simple steps:

1. **Save a digital (electronic) copy of the syllabus on your computer.**

   Save this file somewhere that you can find later, like on your desktop or your My Documents folder (in Windows). This file is most often created with a word processor application, like Word or WordPerfect. You might have gone that extra mile already and created a .pdf file from the original.

2. **Go to your Blackboard Control Panel.**

   If you didn't read the Tip paragraph, about starting at your Control Panel, at the beginning of this chapter, read it now and come back.

3. **In the Content Areas box, select the area in which you want to upload the syllabus.**

   You can simply select the Course Information area in which to place your syllabus. If your institution has customized the default menu so that it doesn't include a Course Information link, choose the most appropriate Content Area for your syllabus. Hey, it might even be a Syllabus link!

4. **Click the Item button on the Add bar near the top of the page.**

   Although the Add Item page has many sections, for quick-start purposes, you need to do only two things: Name the item and upload the file (see Figure 2-1).

5. **Enter the name of your syllabus in the Name text field.**

6. **Scroll down to Section 2 and click the Browse button to find the saved document. Select (highlight) it and click the Open button.**

   Remember where you saved the digital document that's your syllabus? If you need some assistance in performing tasks such as browsing the selection window to find your file, check out a copy of *Windows XP For Dummies,* by Andy Rathbone, or *Macs For Dummies,* by David Pogue (both from Wiley).

Add Item
1 Content Information
Name
Choose Color of Name
Pick
Text
Smart Text
Plain Text
HTML
Preview
2 Content
Files can be attached to the above information. Click Browse to select the file to attach and specify a name for the link to this file.
Attach local file
Browse...
Link to Content Collection item
Browse...
Name of Link to File

Figure 2-1: Add an item to post your syllabus.

7. **Enter an instruction in the Name of Link to File box.**

   Type whatever you want learners to see as a link to the document, such as **Click here to see the syllabus**.

8. **Scroll toward the bottom of the page to Section 4.**

   You can skip past Section 3 for now and try out the Section 3 options later. (If you would rather do them now, though, you have our blessing.)

9. **Click the Submit button.**

   That's it. Easy, isn't it? Congratulations — you posted, or *uploaded,* your syllabus into your Blackboard course! You know that you're successful when you see the receipt page.

Not tired yet? If you really want to do more, click OK to return to the Control Panel so that you can start posting some assignments.

You can also stay in this Content Area and post more items for learners, or even go back to the Control Panel and choose a different Content Area in which to do the same.

Give online assignments

Suppose that you want to post an assignment for learners to turn in (and for you to collect and grade) online. Here's how:

1. **From the Control Panel, select the Content Area link where you want to post the assignment.**

   You can simply select the Assignments area in which to place your assignment. If your institution has customized the default menu so that it doesn't have an Assignments link, choose the most appropriate Content Area for your assignment.

2. **From the drop-down menu on the right side of the Add bar atop the page, select Assignment and click the Go button.**

   Although the Add Assignment screen has several sections, for our purposes in this quick-start guide, we focus on only three specific actions: Name the assignment, give it a point value, and add instructions (see Figure 2-2).

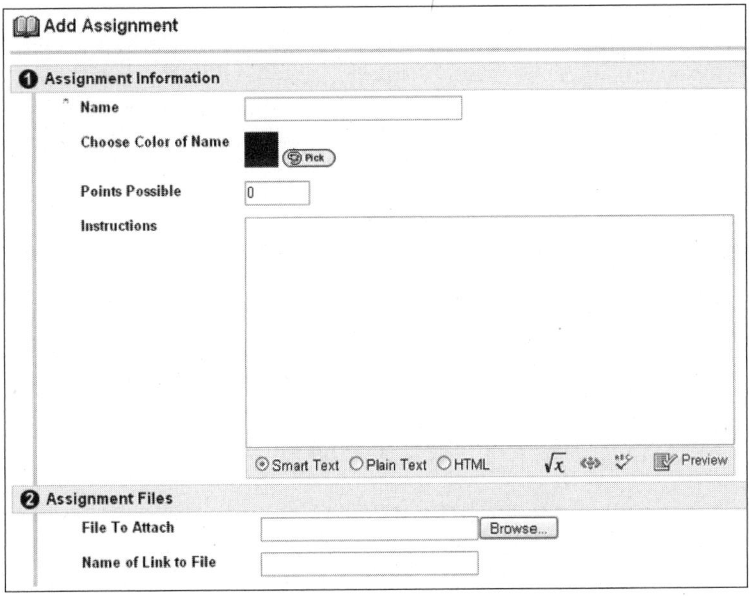

Figure 2-2:
Name your
assignment,
give it a
point value,
and fill in
instructions.

3. **Type the title of the assignment in the Name text box.**

4. **In the Points Possible text box, type — you guessed it! — the maximum number of points a learner can earn on this assignment.**

5. **In the Instructions text box, type (or copy and paste, if the instructions are in another document) the instructions you want learners to see.**

   If the directions for learners are already beautifully displayed in a document (a word processing document or a .pdf file, for example) saved to your computer, continue to Steps 6 and 7. Otherwise, skip to Step 8.

6. **Click the Browse button to find the saved assignment document on your computer, select the document, and click Open.**

7. **In the Name of Link to File text field, enter whatever you want the link to the assignment instructions to say.**

   Type whatever you want learners to see as a link to the document; for example, **Click here to see the homework assignment.**

8. **Click the Submit button.**

   Good job! You gave an online assignment that you can now collect through Blackboard. You know that you're all-powerful when you see the receipt page.

Sharon Widmayer, a high school English teacher from Fairfax County Public Schools, in Virginia, says, "What are my technology skills? Let's say for example, you want to create a quiz with pictures. Do you have a digital camera or a scanner that you know how to use? Do you know how to upload the pictures? My point here is that your great idea may need to be scaled back, at least initially, to what you can easily do and maintain. You want the Blackboard site to be flawless for your students, so it is best to stick to what you can do well rather than risk something not working right or something not finished."

Now that you're on a roll, click OK to return to the Control Panel so that you can set up your Gradebook.

The assignment you just posted now appears as a column title in your Gradebook. Yes, it's that easy.

Set up your Gradebook

Okay, to save time later in your course, it's time to set up Item columns in your Gradebook so that you have to worry only about entering earned points for each learner. Here's what to do:

1. **On the Control Panel, click the Gradebook link in the Assessment pane.**

   You should see your Gradebook in Spreadsheet view (see Figure 2-3). It differs a bit from the View By Student and View By Item options. (We discuss those views in Chapter 9.) The Spreadsheet view displays all your graded items for all learners. Spreadsheet view is a great starting place: It's one-stop shopping for most (if not all) of your grading needs.

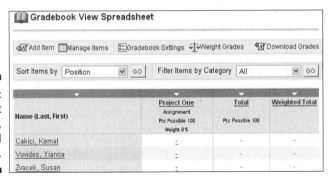

2. **Click the Add Item link.**

   If you added an assignment in the preceding section, it was entered automatically as a Gradebook item. Neat, huh? Now, you can add some other graded items, such as Class Participation or Quiz 1.

3. **Choose the item name, category, and number of possible points.**

   Enter the name of the graded item (Quiz 1 or Homework 2, for example), select the appropriate item type (Exam or Project, for example) from the category drop-down menu, and enter a value (10, 100, or 1000, for example) in the Points Possible field.

4. **Click the Submit button in the lower-right corner of the form.**

5. **Click OK on the receipt page to return to your Gradebook spreadsheet.**

   After you return to the Gradebook spreadsheet, you can add more items, modify item information, or assign grades to learners. We get *much* deeper into the powerful Gradebook tools in Chapter 9.

You might want to start communicating with your learners at this point, even before the course begins.

Mary Bold, PhD, an assistant professor of family studies at Texas Woman's University, says, "Trust your students to be patient with you. Be open and forthright about your novice status in online teaching, and you will enlist student support for each new experiment. In a first semester online, every week qualifies as a new experiment. I remember replying to a student request for grades in the Gradebook in my first semester online: 'Yes, you'll see those grades just as soon as I figure out how to put them there.' Even after mastering the basics of Blackboard, I continue to share experiments with students. In some classes, I build in a menu item called Beta, and that's where I post new efforts, inviting students to give me feedback."

Start discussion topics

Communicating with learners in Blackboard takes several forms. A *discussion* works like an office bulletin board. For this task, you establish a discussion forum and start the conversation as shown in these steps:

1. **On the Blackboard Control Panel, click the Discussion Board link.**

2. **Click the Add Forum button.**

   When you click Add Forum, you see the page shown in Figure 2-4. It sets up a space for you and your learners to trade notes for the rest of the class to view.

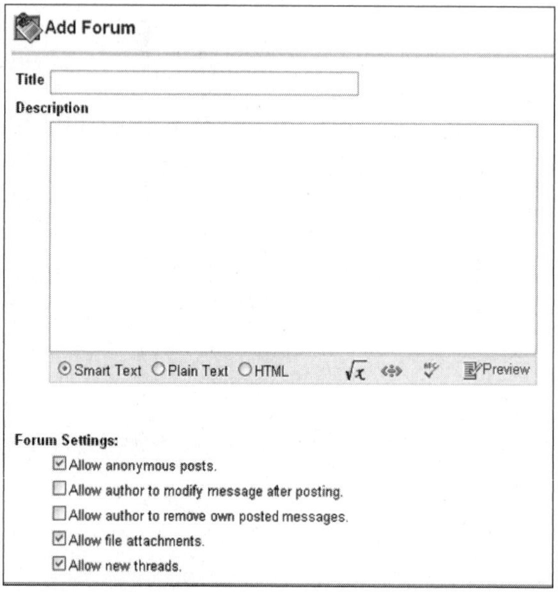

Figure 2-4:
Create a
bulletin
board, also
known as a
Discussion
Forum.

3. **Enter a name for the forum in the Title text field.**

4. **In the Description text box, type a brief explanation of the topic to be discussed in this forum.**

   This text appears below the link (the forum title) for learners to read before proceeding to the messages within this forum.

5. **Enable or disable the check boxes in the Forum Settings field.**

   After you scroll down the page to the next section, you can turn options on or off specifically for this forum. You can find more information about these options in Chapter 4.

6. **Click the Submit button to create the forum.**

7. **Click OK on the receipt page that appears.**

   This action returns you to the Discussion Forums page. After you create the forum, your next task is to post the first note to which you want learners to reply.

8. **Click the forum name you just created to enter this topic area.**

9. **Click the Add New Thread button.**

   Now that you're inside the forum you created, the conversation can begin.

10. **Enter the subject in the Subject text field, and the message in the Message text box.**

    This is your first message to the class of learners who will read this discussion forum.

11. **Click the Submit button.**

    Figure 2-5 shows you what your initial message looks like on the board inside the forum, after a learner posts a reply.

Figure 2-5:
Look —
signs of life
in your
course!

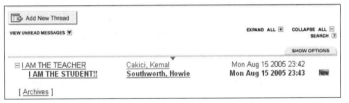

Kevin Dunn, chef instructor of advanced food preparation at Grand Rapids Community College, says, "I used Blackboard to help with the continuity. My students are required to use Blackboard each week. I grade them on their Discussion Boards as they relate to external links and new topics of interest. I also utilize photos in a large way through my Blackboard course. I have students critique their own food plating. This improves the overall plating performance and culinary skills."

The bridge

Now that you have (or haven't) read about what a quick-start guide can do for you, the remainder of this chapter is dedicated to giving you a slightly more in-depth look at how to nurture a course from sapling to sprawling supertree with succulent fruit, powerful branches, and enormous leaves — wait. This description seems extreme, and perhaps overly colorful, but the remainder of this chapter does tell you how to create a truly elegant course from the bottom up. If reading the quick-start guide made you say "I got it," reading the rest of this chapter will make you say "Now I *really* get it."

Figure 2-6 outlines the Before, During, and After stages of a traditional course-development process. Basically, you begin by spreading the seeds of a course and end by sharing the fruit across terms and semesters.

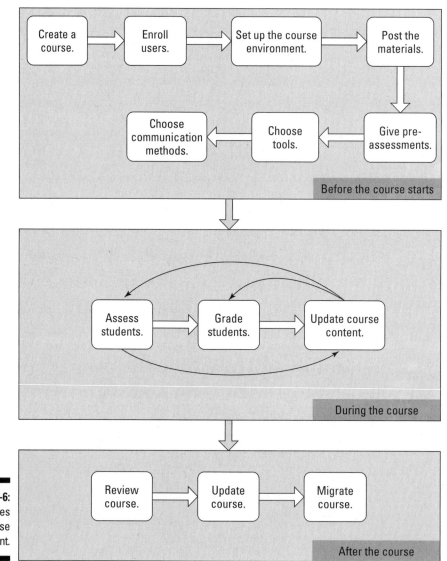

Figure 2-6:
The stages
of course
development.

Starting a Brand-New Course

"Where, oh, where should I begin a Blackboard course?" This is the age-old question. Or, is it "Which came first, Black or the Board?" Whichever the question, the answer, we believe, is the same: Everything starts from the beginning. Start by making the space, continue by filling that space with things, and round it all out by putting the filled-up space to good use. Our first stage in the course-development process, in certain terms, is to build your course from scratch.

Before we get started, we have to mention (again) that all the steps in this section assume that you're already logged in to Blackboard and are looking at the Control Panel in one of your courses. Refer to Chapter 1, which holds all the secrets of getting here. In truth, there's not a whole lot of magic in Chapter 1, but it definitely gives you the 411 about how you can go about getting yourself into Blackboard and navigating easily around it.

1. **Create a course.**

   In this step (see Figure 2-7), some institutions automatically generate courses for their instructors, some create Blackboard courses by request, and others let instructors create their own Blackboard courses. Many institutions use a combination of these approaches, based on the types of courses being created.

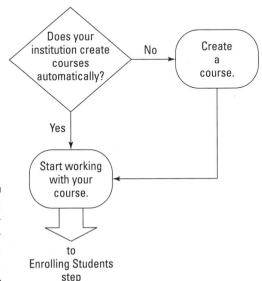

Figure 2-7:
Your choices for creating a course.

2. Enroll users.

See Figure 2-8 for a sample visual representation of the enrollment process. For a deep understanding of the Blackboard enrollment features, see Chapter 3.

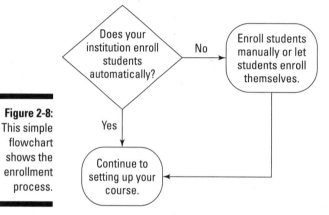

Figure 2-8:
This simple flowchart shows the enrollment process.

Depending on how Blackboard is set up at your institution, you, as an instructor, might enroll learners by clicking the Enroll Users link from your course Control Panel to display the Enroll Users page (see Figure 2-9). Some institutions require learners to enroll themselves in courses, or the institution might enroll learners automatically in the Blackboard courses in which they're already registered with the school.

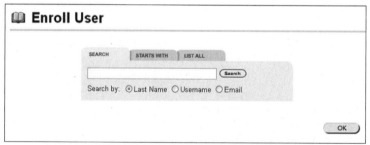

Figure 2-9:
Enrolling users, if you need to, is as easy as pie.

Your Blackboard system administrator is your best friend. Ask her how learners get into your course on Blackboard.

One creative and quick way to view current enrollments in your course is to click the Gradebook link on the Control Panel. Even if no grades are entered, you see all your learners' names.

3. Set up the course environment.

You can customize your course menu based on what learners need to do in the course, and what kind of information they need to access and interact with. Yes, that's right: You can add menu items, take some away, and even alter the colors that learners see onscreen. You customize menu items from the course Control Panel (see Figure 2-10) by using the Manage Course Menu link (see Figure 2-11). Chapter 4 covers all the steps involved in customizing the course menu.

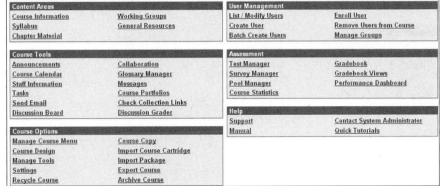

Figure 2-10:
The all-
powerful
Course
Control
Panel.

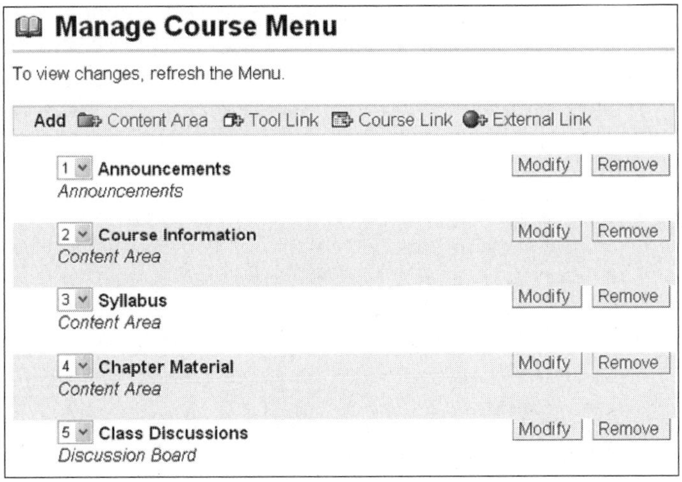

Figure 2-11:
Monkeying
with your
course
menu.

4. Post course material.

You're likely to post most of your course materials by using the Add bar (see Figure 2-12) within any Content Area page. You can post your syllabus, readings, documents, photos, or spreadsheets, for example. From the Control Panel, you click the Content Area link in which you want to add some materials. Chapter 5 gives you all the grand details of how to use Content Areas to their fullest.

Figure 2-12:
Putting
materials
into Content
Areas.

Blackboard provides folders and learning units to help you stay organized. Within them, you can arrange your content according to class sessions, lectures, tutorials, or topics.

5. Give pre-assessments.

Finding out what your learners already know when they start your course allows you to gauge your introductory overview of the course content. The following Blackboard tools help you do that. Chapter 6 gives you detailed steps for using these tools:

- **Discussion Board:** Gather responses from learners by using a Discussion Forum. Using discussions, you can choose to run an anonymous or named online back-and-forth conversation.

- **Survey Manager:** Whether you want to carry out a quick two-question poll or conduct a ten-question survey, the Survey Manager is a powerful tool to gather this type of data about your class. All surveys are anonymous.

- **Assignment:** Use a nongraded assignment to find out what learners already know about the subject. Or, you can use a graded assignment and really freak them out. (Kidding.)

- **Test Manager:** Give learners a test as soon as they start the course? Isn't that barbaric? Or, is it insight into a learner's mind to help you teach more effectively or better begin your first class session? Only you can decide!

6. Choose the proper tools for your course.

Blackboard offers a variety of tools to help you as an instructor and a set of tools to help learners take away something from the course. Think of the Course Tools as teaching and learning support. (By the way, you can access these tools, some of which are shown in Figure 2-13, from the Blackboard Control Panel.)

📖 Tool Availability

Tool	Available	Allow Guest	Allow Observer
Address Book Address Book	☑	●	☐
Announcements Announcements	☑	☐	☑
Adaptive Release Adaptive Release	☑	●	●

Figure 2-13: Choose your Course Tools.

Before starting a course, consider what you're going to do to keep the course moving along smoothly. Perhaps you're using the Course Calendar to help your learners manage their time? Maybe you're using the Tasks tool to accomplish the same goal? Chapters 6 and 7 apply a full-court press to uses and abuses of the Course Tools.

If you plan to use a tool, such as Calendar or Tasks, to help your learners along the path to enlightenment, include it on the course menu. See Chapter 4 for the grand details.

7. **Choose your communication methods.**

Blackboard offers the following communication tools (see Chapter 6) that you can use to facilitate both one-way and two-way communication for interaction that's either *synchronous* (in real time, like on a phone) or *asynchronous* (*not* in real time, like on a bulletin board).

- **Discussion Board:** Post ideas, questions, and theories, and allow learners to do the same. All responses can be viewed by everyone in the class, or by specific groups reading the Discussion Board (see Figure 2-14).

- **Collaboration (or chat room):** Use this tool to allow learners to connect with each other synchronously (at the same time).

- **Send Email:** Send messages to all users, some users, or one user from within Blackboard.

Many institutions require their learners to use only their institutional e-mail addresses in order to use the Blackboard e-mail communication features, and other institutions allow learners to use any e-mail address (such as AOL, Hotmail, Yahoo, or Gmail, for example).

- **Messages:** Send notes to the whole class, and receive messages from class members. This feature is really just like e-mail. Yet, these messages are internal to Blackboard, which means that learners don't have to divulge their e-mail addresses to receive and send messages. This option isn't available in the Basic edition.

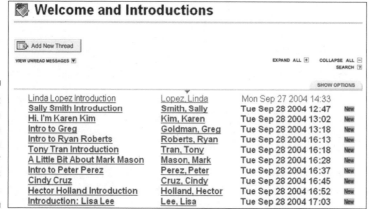

Figure 2-14: An example of using the Discussion Boards for class introductions.

Before starting your course, think about the selection of the communication tools that you and your learners will use during the course and for what purpose, and make these expectations clear to your learners. It's also a great idea to simply tell your learners how you will, and will not, use the Blackboard communications features.

Again, Chapter 6 fully describes the options and steps in setting up and using these communication tools.

Facilitating a Course

Blackboard provides features to help you spend your time efficiently during the life of the course. The process of seeing a course through to its end involves a few tried and true teaching tasks:

1. **Assess learners.**

   Several features in Blackboard allow you, the instructor, to create both formative and summative assessments. See Chapter 8 for detailed steps for using these tools:

   - **Test Manager:** Use this tool to create practice tests or graded tests.

   - **Survey Manager:** Create anonymous surveys that provide insight into knowledge gaps and learner satisfaction about your course.

- **Pool Manager:** Create *question pools* that allow you to compile tests of varying questions across the class and to offer a flexible way to create make-up tests.

- **Assignment tool:** Go totally paperless, from paperless assignment submission to paperless instructor feedback (see Figure 2-15). To make life even easier, the Assignment feature is also connected to the Gradebook feature.

- **Discussion Boards:** Set up a collaborative environment for assessment. It can be in the form of peer reviews or self-assessments, for example.

Figure 2-15:
Finally,
home-
work is
graded the
easy way.

📖 Add Assignment
❶ **Assignment Information**

Name — HOMEWORK #1

Choose Color of Name — (🎨 Pick)

Points Possible — 100

Instructions — Normal | 3 | Times New Roman | **B** *I* U ...
<HTML> Preview

PLEASE DO THIS WITHOUT THE HELP OF YOUR TEXT BOOK!

Thanks,

Teacher.

2. Provide feedback about learner progress.

The Blackboard Gradebook helps instructors manage all the grades involved in a course (see Figure 2-16). On the learner side, the Blackboard My Grades page allows learners to see all their grades for the course.

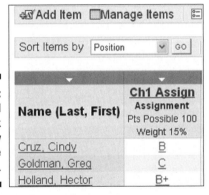

Figure 2-16:
A small
sneak
preview
of the
Gradebook.

Name (Last, First)	Ch1 Assign Assignment Pts Possible 100 Weight 15%
Cruz, Cindy	B
Goldman, Greg	C
Holland, Hector	B+

Add Item / Manage Items

Sort Items by Position GO

The tools described in Step 1 are integrated with the Gradebook so that if you use the Test Manager to include a test in your course, a column is automatically created in your Blackboard Gradebook that allows you to enter grades and do much more. You can also provide feedback to learners for assignments that use the Assignment tool by either typing your comments or attaching a file.

The flexibility of the Gradebook in Blackboard makes it a must-use tool for course facilitation. The Gradebook helps you keep track of the grades you give and provides learners with a clear summary of how they're doing in your course.

Again, Chapter 9 outlines the Gradebook functionalities and how to use them.

If you use objective question types (true/false, multiple choice, or ordering, for example) on a test created and administered through Blackboard, the Blackboard system grades those questions automatically based on the number of points you determine each question is worth.

Third-party test-preparation software and question banks are available that plug into Blackboard. We recommend that you contact the publishers of your favorite textbooks because many larger companies now have Blackboard-friendly question sets.

3. **Update course content.**

During course facilitation, as you may have already discovered, you must update your course content — whether you modify existing content, add new content, or remove content. Blackboard offers you the ability to change any content item that you include in your course by providing the following buttons, which appear next to each item you add:

- **Modify:** Change some aspect of the item's text, point value, or questions, for example.

- **Copy:** Duplicate the item or move it to a different area of the same course or another course that you're teaching.

- **Remove:** Just get rid of the item already!

Changing or updating content might confuse learners or throw them off track. Be sure to communicate with your learners if you alter anything about your course in midstream.

Ending the Party: Life in the After-Course

The *After* phase of a course is a tough one on the instructor. You have no more homework to grade, no more virtual spitballs to dodge, and no more whining to endure. Wait — those are the good things about the After stage. Whew! After you're done using a Blackboard course for a term or semester, you have a chance to breathe in the aroma of freshly baked course evaluations, take stock in the academic life, and regenerate, because you must do it all again very soon. The following list of tasks to complete should make life in the "after-course" less macabre than it sounds:

1. **Review your course.**

   After the course is over, you should review the course itself, by basing your review on learner course evaluations and your own reflections about the success of the course. You might want to take on updates as a project and keep notes for yourself throughout a term so that when the course has ended, you locate your notes and update them in one fell swoop.

2. **Update the course.**

   When you update your course, consider creating a master course as a template for future offerings of the same course. If you already have a master course, be sure to update the master based on the review action items (refer to Step 1).

   Remember to keep a record of learner work and grades. You can do this by downloading your Gradebook and either printing or saving files submitted by your learners throughout the course. We tell you how to do that in Chapter 9.

3. **Migrate the course.**

   Blackboard offers several ways to migrate a course for reuse: Course Copy, Export Course (coupled with Import Package), and Archive Course. Using the Course Copy feature (see Figure 2-17) is by far the simplest option if you intend to reuse your course within the same institution.

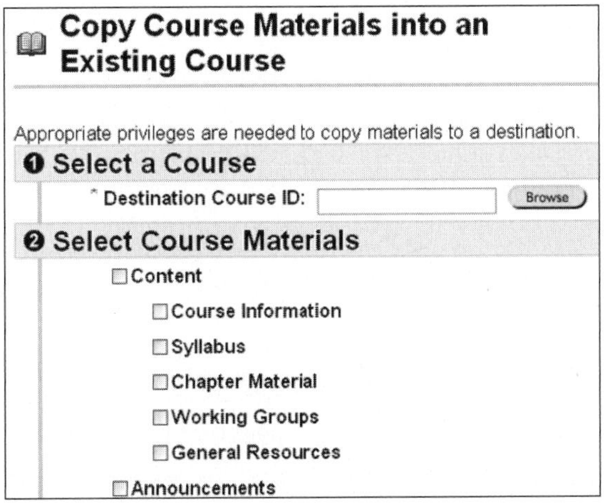

Figure 2-17:
Copy only
what you
need.

> ### 📖 Copy Course Materials into an Existing Course
>
> Appropriate privileges are needed to copy materials to a destination.
>
> **❶ Select a Course**
>
> * Destination Course ID: [＿＿＿＿＿＿] (Browse)
>
> **❷ Select Course Materials**
>
> ☐ Content
> ☐ Course Information
> ☐ Syllabus
> ☐ Chapter Material
> ☐ Working Groups
> ☐ General Resources
> ☐ Announcements

The Export Course feature produces a compressed (.zip) file with all course materials that can be saved on your computer, CD-ROM, USB key, thumb drive, or other type of removable media. Your intention might be to take your course with you to another institution (that uses Blackboard). We cover all these course-management features in Chapter 10.

Your institution might take care of copying, exporting, and archiving courses for you, in which case these options might not be available to you. Check with your Blackboard System Administrator to find out who's responsible for taking care of these tasks. Remember your best friend!

When you export a compressed (.zip) file, make sure that your removable storage device or computer has enough space on it to save the file. When you use Export Course, the download link lists a file size next to it.

Part II
Easing into Blackboard

The 5th Wave   By Rich Tennant

"Okay, well, I think we all get the gist of where Jerry was going with the site map."

In this part . . .

We would bet that you're reading this book because you want to create a Blackboard course five minutes ago, right? Well, this section focuses on the "how-to" of that process — all the button clicks and fill-in-the-blanks that get you an online learning environment full of all the essential elements!

Chapter 3 introduces the steps for managing your list of learners, from adding and removing them from the course to putting them into project groups. If your institution does this work for you, you're off the hook.

Chapter 4 discusses changing the look of your Blackboard course and choosing the tools that will engage learners with your course in a meaningful way. This chapter is really about structure and matching your Blackboard course to your instructional needs and style.

Chapter 5 gets right to the heart of the matter: your course content. For many instructors, putting course materials (notes, graphics, and readings, for example) online is a great place to start with a Blackboard course. If that's true of you, get a move on!

In Chapter 6, you'll find step-by-step instructions for the many communication options in Blackboard. If one of your goals is to get students talking — ideally, about your course content — run, don't walk, to this chapter and try out the tools for interaction.

What are you waiting for? Pick a chapter and start clicking!

Chapter 3

Got Learners?
(Getting People into Your Course)

In This Chapter

▶ Keeping track of learners' access to your course

▶ Enhancing the collaborative experience

*W*hat would your course be without students? It would be perhaps a chance for you to teach yourself something, but we wouldn't recommend Blackboard for that! Whether you're presenting a course for students or the workforce, Blackboard makes getting learners up and going quickly a fairly easy task. This chapter takes you through the process of creating users (students, instructors, and teaching assistants, for example) in your Blackboard system and adding them to your course. After you create them in the course, you can also group them for projects and the like.

"Manage my own users? Get out of town! I don't even see them on my Control Panel!" If you read the first half of this chapter and sound like this, just stick with us. Some schools lock instructors out of these functions because enrollment is done either automatically or by system administrators who are locked away in a lonely towers (or, usually, basements). It sounds scary, but it saves you some work if you're one of those lucky ones.

Managing Learner Accounts

In this section, you find instructions for managing the user accounts for the Blackboard course you're setting up. We walk you through the process of creating user accounts, enrolling users in your course, assigning roles to users, and removing users from the roster. Ready, set, go!

To get started, go to your Blackboard course and choose Control Panel from the course menu. All the functions you need for managing user accounts are in the User Management pane of the Control Panel (see Figure 3-1).

Figure 3-1: Control Panel — your gateway to managing your course.

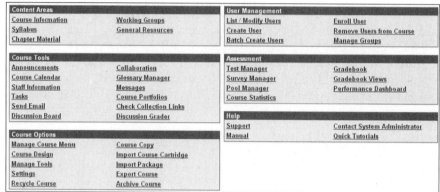

Content Areas		User Management	
Course Information	Working Groups	List / Modify Users	Enroll User
Syllabus	General Resources	Create User	Remove Users from Course
Chapter Material		Batch Create Users	Manage Groups
Course Tools		**Assessment**	
Announcements	Collaboration	Test Manager	Gradebook
Course Calendar	Glossary Manager	Survey Manager	Gradebook Views
Staff Information	Messages	Pool Manager	Performance Dashboard
Tasks	Course Portfolios	Course Statistics	
Send Email	Check Collection Links		
Discussion Board	Discussion Grader	**Help**	
Course Options		Support	Contact System Administrator
Manage Course Menu	Course Copy	Manual	Quick Tutorials
Course Design	Import Course Cartridge		
Manage Tools	Import Package		
Settings	Export Course		
Recycle Course	Archive Course		

Don't be surprised if your institution doesn't allow you to create accounts — most don't (for all sorts of reasons). However, if this capability is available to you, you need to know how to use it. Follow these steps:

1. **Click the Create User link in the User Management pane of the Control Panel.**

   Not surprisingly, this step takes you to the Create User page, where you build this user's account. Four sections are on this page:

   - Personal Information

   - Account Information

   - Personal Information (yes, a second one)

   - Role and Availability

2. **Enter the user's first name, last name, e-mail address, and student ID in the corresponding fields in Section 1.**

   Although only first and last names are designated as required fields, you want to include the e-mail address so that you can send e-mail by using Blackboard. You might also be expected to include a student ID to avoid confusion between users with the same names.

3. **Enter a username for this individual in Section 2.**

Your institution might have a standard template for creating usernames (for example, first initial followed by last name), or you might be allowed to create your own.

4. Enter the password for the user to access the Blackboard course.

5. Reenter the password for verification (see Figure 3-2).

When you type the password, bullets appear rather than the characters you type.

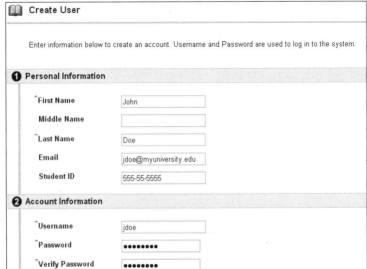

Figure 3-2:
Creating a
new user
account —
personal
and account
information
sections.

6. In Section 3 of the page, determine which fields you want (or need) to fill in and enter the appropriate information for Section 3.

None of these areas is required in order to create a user account, but your institution might expect you to fill in some of them for other reasons.

7. Click the appropriate radio button next to the role the user will play in the course.

The default role is Student. We cover the other roles a few pages down the road. (Feel free to peek ahead, if you're curious.)

8. Choose Yes or No from the drop-down menu under the line Available (This Course Only).

Choosing Yes, as shown in Figure 3-3, makes the account available to the user immediately. Choosing No creates the account, but it remains unavailable to the user until you activate it.

Figure 3-3:
Deciding on
a student's
role and
course
availability.

9. **Click the Submit button.**

   The next screen you see confirms the addition of this account by providing, under the heading List/Modify Users, a summary of the user information that has been added.

10. **Click the OK button.**

    You return to the Create User page, where you can create more users, if you like.

Creating users in this way does two things at a time: creates the user account and enrolls that user in your course. So, after you complete this step, you can skip right over the next section, which talks about enrolling users, because you've already done it.

To return to the Control Panel, click the Cancel button (in the lower-right corner) or click the Control Panel link in the bread crumb trail at the top of the screen.

Enrolling Users

Although few instructors are expected to create user accounts, there's a greater chance that you need to enroll users in your Blackboard course. To *enroll* simply means that you provide users who already have accounts on the Blackboard system with access to the course, whether they're students or teaching assistants or are filling some other role in your course. Follow these steps:

1. **From the Control Panel, click the Enroll User link in the User Management pane.**

This step brings up a rather empty-looking page, where you can search for the user you want to add.

2. **Enter the last name of the user in the corresponding text field and click the Search button.**

   Blackboard generates a list of system users (everyone who has an account within this Blackboard system) with that last name, from which you can select the appropriate individual to add to your site (see Figure 3-4).

   For common names, the list might extend across two or more pages. Use the bread crumbs in the lower-left corner of the page to move to the next set of users.

Figure 3-4:
Searching
for a user
among all
Blackboard
accounts.

You can search instead by username or e-mail address, if you want. This capability can be useful in narrowing your search if a user has a common last name. To search by username or e-mail address, simply click the appropriate radio button on the Search By line and enter the username or e-mail address.

3. **Click to enable the check box to the left of the user's name in the list, and then click the Submit button.**

   The next screen you see (labeled Receipt: Success) tells you that this individual is enrolled in your course with the role of Student (see Figure 3-5).

4. **Click the OK button to return to the Control Panel.**

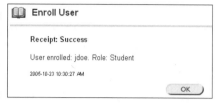

Figure 3-5:
Confirming a
successful
transaction.

Enroll User

Receipt: Success

User enrolled: jdoe. Role: Student

2005-10-23 10:30:27 AM

OK

If you attempt to enroll an individual who is already listed in your Blackboard course roster, the system (unfortunately) doesn't inform you. Rather than tell you, "Hey, Sherlock, this person is already on the roster!" the system simply doesn't find the account. So, if you search and can't find someone, check to make sure that he's not already included on the roster.

"Who's in My Course?"

How can you tell whether someone is on the course roster? Start at the Control Panel, of course. To get there, choose Control Panel from the course menu and follow these steps:

1. **Click the List/Modify Users link.**

   This step displays a page similar to the Enroll User page, with a field you can use to search for a specific individual on your course roster.

2a. **Enter the user's last name (or username or e-mail address) in the field and click the Search button.**

   This step generates a list of everyone with that last name on your course roster.

2b. **Alternatively, to list the entire roster rather than only one person, click the List All tab, above the Search field.**

   The note on the List All tab warns you that processing a large class might take a while. Are you patient? Determined to see the entire roster?

3. **Click the List All button.**

   The names appear in alphabetical order by last name, with 25 names per page. The total number of users appears at the beginning of the list, and additional information (username, e-mail address, and role, for example) also appears for each name on the list.

Did you notice the Password and Properties buttons by the names on your roster? You probably don't need to mess with the Password button, but the Properties option is helpful in the next section, which talks about assigning user roles.

4. Click the OK button to return to the Control Panel.

You might notice that because you didn't change anything in your Blackboard course and were simply viewing the roster, you don't see a Receipt screen confirming your actions.

Deciding on a User's Role

Was it Shakespeare who said, "Blackboard is a stage and each must play a part"? Okay, maybe not exactly, but it's true that everyone has a part to play in any Blackboard course in which they're participating. The role might be that of Course Builder, Grader, Guest, Instructor, Student, or Teaching Assistant. Each role carries a specific set of privileges and capabilities, which might be customized by a system administrator. As an instructor, you can assign roles to the users in your course site, to provide varying levels of access to the course.

1. Go to the Control Panel (choose Control Panel from the course menu) and click the List/Modify Users link (in the User Management pane).

This link is the same one you would use to view the full roster, or to search for a specific user on the roster.

2. Enter the last name of the person whose role you want to change and then click the Search button.

You can also search by username or e-mail address by clicking the appropriate radio button (on the Search By line) and entering that information rather than the last name. A list of users enrolled in the course site with that last name (or username or e-mail address) appears.

Here's a shortcut for the multiple steps involved in using the List All feature. If you simply click the Search button without typing anything in the Search text field, you see a list of all users in the system.

3. Click the Properties button to the right of the user's name.

The next screen you see displays areas labeled Personal Information, Account Information, and Role and Availability data for this user (see Figure 3-6).

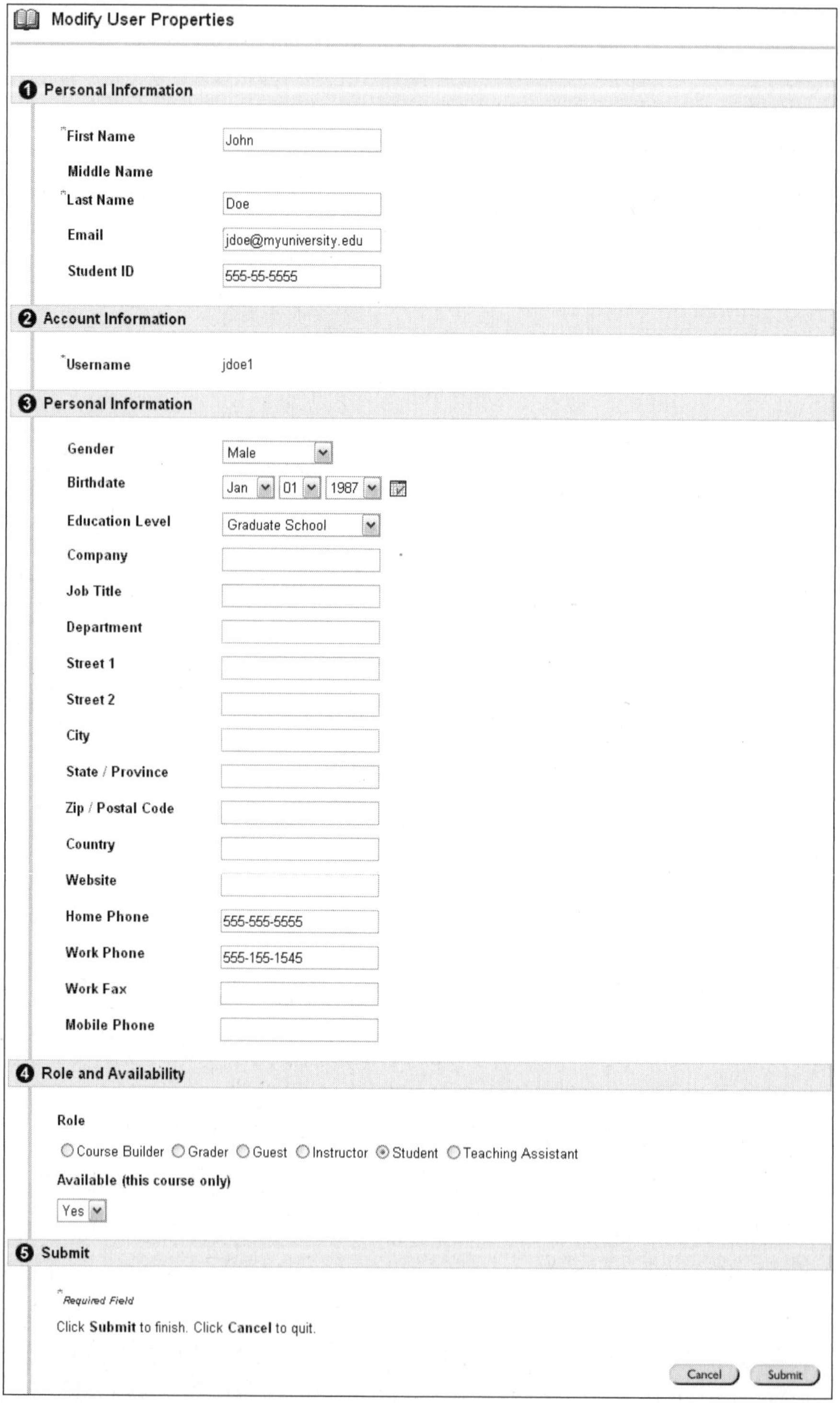

📖 Modify User Properties

❶ Personal Information

"First Name   John

Middle Name

"Last Name   Doe

Email   jdoe@myuniversity.edu

Student ID   555-55-5555

❷ Account Information

"Username   jdoe1

❸ Personal Information

Gender   Male

Birthdate   Jan ▾ 01 ▾ 1987 ▾ 📝

Education Level   Graduate School ▾

Company

Job Title

Department

Street 1

Street 2

City

State / Province

Zip / Postal Code

Country

Website

Home Phone   555-555-5555

Work Phone   555-155-1545

Work Fax

Mobile Phone

❹ Role and Availability

Role

○ Course Builder ○ Grader ○ Guest ○ Instructor ⦿ Student ○ Teaching Assistant

Available (this course only)

Yes ▾

❺ Submit

"Required Field

Click **Submit** to finish. Click **Cancel** to quit.

Cancel   Submit

Figure 3-6:
Modifying
user
properties.

4. **Go to Section 4, Role and Availability, and click the radio button beside the role you want to assign to this user (see Figure 3-7).**

Figure 3-7:
Assigning
roles and
availability
to users.

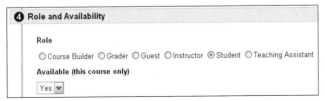

Although privileges assigned to specific roles might be customized by the system administrator, this list shows you the initial access-level settings:

- **Student:** All content areas and tools enabled by the instructor.

- **Instructor:** All areas of the Control Panel. Go to town!

- **Teaching Assistant (TA):** Has almost the same abilities as the instructor except that the TA isn't listed in the Course Catalog listing for the course.

- **Course Builder:** Control Panel, *except for* the Gradebook and Course Statistics.

- **Grader:** Includes the Control Panel, but *only* within the User Management, Assessment, and Help panes and selected areas of the Course Tools pane.

- **Guest:** Includes announcements, Content Areas, staff information only, and selected content enabled by the instructor.

The system administrator can change some of the privileges for these roles. Check with her if a role doesn't have access to a tool or area it might need.

5. **Choose Yes or No from the drop-down menu below the line labeled Available (This Course Only).**

Choosing Yes enables this user to access the course site immediately, with the privileges accorded the assigned role. Choosing No disables user access to the course site until it's changed by the instructor, teaching assistant, or system administrator.

6. **Click the Submit button.**

The next screen you see confirms the changes to this user's account, by providing a summary of the account information, under the heading List/Modify Users.

7. **Click OK to return to the List/Modify Users page.**

   Start with Step 1 to change another user's role, or click OK again to return to the Control Panel.

Removing Users

Removing users from your course roster is even easier than adding them, and might prove useful if (heaven forbid!) someone drops your course or needs to be removed for other reasons. Removing a user from the roster doesn't delete his Blackboard account from the system; it merely discontinues his access to your Blackboard course site. Follow these steps to remove a user from your course:

1. **Go to the Control Panel (if you're not already there, choose Control Panel from the course menu) and click the Remove Users from Course link in the User Management pane.**

   You see the text `Remove Users from Course` and a box where you can enter the user's name.

2a. **Type the user's last name in the box and click the Search button.**

   You can also search by username or e-mail address by clicking the appropriate radio button (on the Search By line) and entering that information rather than the last name. A list of users with that last name (or username or e-mail address) who are enrolled in the course site appears.

2b. **Alternatively, to remove more than one user at a time, clicking the Search button without entering anything in the Search text field makes sense. This step displays all users in your course.**

   If you have a large enrollment class, the list of users might take a while to appear.

3. **When the names of the users to be removed appear, select the check boxes to the left of the names (see Figure 3-8).**

   Only 25 names are displayed at a time, so if your class size is large, use the page number buttons at the bottom of the screen to view more usernames.

   You have to submit your selections one page at a time before going to the next page.

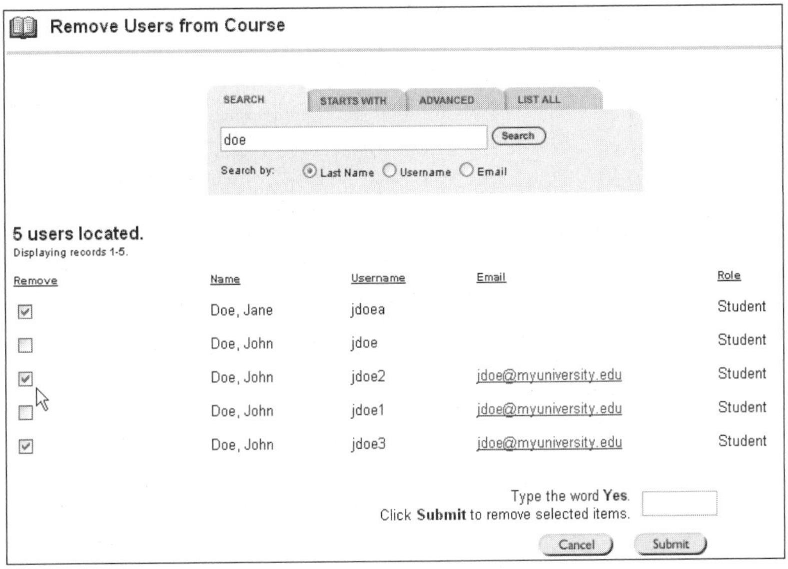

Figure 3-8:
Removing
users from a
course.

4. **Type the word** Yes **in the box at the bottom of the page.**

   Type it exactly the way you see it here, not yes or YES. If you type the
   word incorrectly, an error message shows up to remind you to enter Yes
   in the box.

5. **Click the Submit button.**

   Blackboard warns you that "this action is final and cannot be undone."
   Be sure that you really mean to delete the user's name you checked,
   because any scores entered for that person in the Gradebook disappear
   after they're removed from the course roster.

6. **If you're sure, click the OK button.**

   The Receipt: Success screen then displays a list of users who were
   removed. Click OK to return to the Control Panel.

Managing Groups

Blackboard allows you to set up groups within your course site and provide
each group with a set of communication tools (file exchange, discussion
boards, chat, and e-mail) that are accessible only by the group's members. In
this two-part process, you first create the group shell, or *environment,* and
enable the tools and then assign users to the group.

Back to the Control Panel! To get there, choose Control Panel from the course menu and follow these steps:

1. Click the Manage Groups link in the User Management pane.

The next screen you see shows the groups that have already been created in this site. Because you're just beginning, however, this page looks rather bare.

2. Click the Add Group button.

The page that's displayed has three sections: Group Information, Group Options, and Submit (see Figure 3-9).

3. Enter a name for the group in the Name text box.

You can simply give these groups placeholder names for now and let students in each group come up with their own names. In any case, avoid using numbers or letters that can be perceived negatively. Would *you* want to be in Group F, for example?

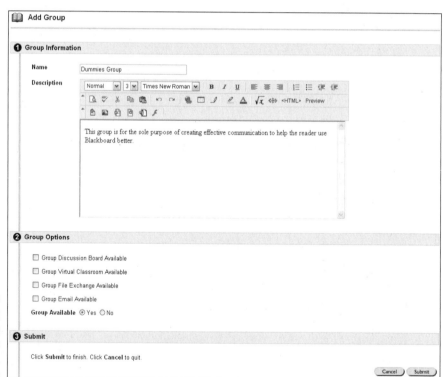

Figure 3-9:
Adding groups to your course.

4. **Enter descriptive information or other text in the Description box, underneath the Name field.**

This step is optional, although it might prove useful later when you're trying to remember which group has what topic or project.

5. **In Section 2 (see Figure 3-10), select the tools you want to enable for this group.**

Figure 3-10: Selecting the collaborative tools a group is allowed to use.

Group Options

☐ Group Discussion Board Available

☐ Group Virtual Classroom Available

☐ Group File Exchange Available

☐ Group Email Available

Group Available ⦿ Yes ○ No

Select the check box next to each tool you want to enable (Discussion Board, Virtual Classroom, File Exchange, or Email, for example).

If you enable the discussion board for a group, you (as the instructor) also have to go back and set up a forum in which group members can interact. Group members cannot use the discussion board until you do this task because they, as students, don't have the right to establish a forum in a discussion board. (From Display view or Student view in the course, choose Communication⇨Group Pages⇨Group Name Link⇨ Group Discussion Board⇨Add Forum; see Chapter 6 for more information about these options.)

Repeat this step for any group that uses the discussion board.

6. **Select Yes or No to make the groups and group tools available to the members.**

Selecting Yes means that as soon as a student is added to a group, she has access to the tools that were enabled in the preceding step. Selecting No prevents access to groups and tools until an instructor, teaching assistant, or system administrator enables them.

7. **Click the Submit button to create the group.**

The Receipt: Success page confirms that the group has been added.

8. **Click the OK button to return to the Manage Groups page.**

You can then create another group or assign users to any group that's created.

Adding users to a group

After you create the group environment (refer to the preceding section), you have to add the students in the group. To do this, first choose Control Panel from the course menu and click the Manage Groups link in the User Management pane. Then, follow these steps:

1. **Click the Modify button to the right of the group name.**

   You see four options:

   • Group Properties

   • Add Users to Group

   • List Users in Group

   • Remove Users from Group

2. **Click the Add Users to Group link.**

   You see a search box in which you can enter a user's name and an option to display the full roster.

3. **To see the entire roster, click the Search button without entering anything in the Search text field.**

   This action lists all users in your course (25 per page).

4. **To add a user to this group, select the check box to the left of the user's name (see Figure 3-11).**

   You can add to the group as many of the users on this page as you want. If no users are listed on the first page you want to assign to this group, use the page number buttons at the bottom of the screen to move ahead in the roster.

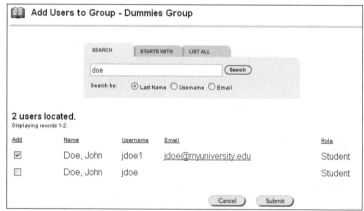

Figure 3-11:
Adding
users to a
group.

Submit names one page at a time.

5. **Click the Submit button.**

   The Receipt: Success screen indicates that you have successfully added the user to the group.

6. **Click OK to return to the list of options for this group.**

   You can add more group members or modify the group in other ways. If you want to add members to a different group, click OK to return to the list of groups you established in your Blackboard course.

Listing users in a group

You might want to see a list of users you included in a particular group. Follow these steps to do this task from the Control Panel (if you're not there, first choose Control Panel from the course menu):

1. **Click the Manage Groups link in the User Management pane.**

   After you establish some groups, the group names are displayed when you click the Manage Groups link.

2. **Click the Modify button to the right of the group name.**

   Four options are displayed:

   - Group Properties
   - Add Users to Group
   - List Users in Group
   - Remove Users from Group

3. **Click the List Users in Group link.**

   You can then search for a specific group member by name or display all group members by name.

4. **Click the List All tab to see all members in the group.**

   Blackboard warns you that, if you have a large class, this step could take a while.

5. **Click the List All button.**

   Blackboard displays the group roster, alphabetically by last name, along with the username, e-mail address, and course role for each group member.

6. **Click OK to return to the Manage Group options page.**

   Click OK once more to go back to the list of all groups within this Blackboard course.

Removing users from a group

If students switch from one group to another, you have to remove them from the initial group and add them to the second. To remove someone from a specific group, start from the Control Panel and follow these steps:

1. **Click the Manage Groups link (in the User Management pane).**

   A list of all groups shows up on the page that's displayed.

2. **Click the Modify button to the right of the group name.**

   Four options are displayed:

   - Group Properties
   - Add Users to Group
   - List Users in Group
   - Remove Users from Group

3. **Click the Remove Users from Group link.**

   On the next page that's displayed, you can search for a specific group member by last name, username, or e-mail address or display all group members' names.

4. **Click the Search button without typing anything in the Search text field.**

   Blackboard displays the group roster, alphabetically by last name, along with the username, e-mail address, and course role for each group member.

5. **Click the box to the left of the group member to be removed.**

   Make sure that a check mark appears in the box when you click it.

6. **Type the word** Yes **in the empty box in the lower-right corner of the page.**

   Blackboard is fussy about this step. Typing YES doesn't work, nor does yes. It accepts only Yes.

7. **Click the Submit button.**

   Blackboard warns you that removing someone from a group is serious business. Make sure that you select the right name.

8. **Click the OK button.**

   Blackboard confirms that you were successful in removing this user from the group.

9. **Click OK again to return to the Manage Course options page.**

   To return to the list of groups, click OK one more time. If you've read this main section and already know how to add a user to a group, you're set.

Chapter 4

Making the Course Your Own

In This Chapter

▶ Dealing with the course menu

▶ Playing well with the tools

*S*uccess in gaining and keeping learner attention in a Blackboard course is highly dependent on your course structure and the choices you make in building it.

The course menu is one of the main elements in your Blackboard course that communicates what you feel is important for your learners to access easily and often throughout the course. The course menu is your learners' main navigation system into your course content. For example, students need to refer to the syllabus repeatedly throughout the course, even though you review it with them early in the course. Therefore, giving the syllabus its own menu item makes sense.

To use any of the features we describe in this chapter, you should start at your course Control Panel (ah, yes, an instructor's springboard into Blackboard adventure!). Follow these steps to get there:

1. **Log in to Blackboard by using your username and password.**

   Assuming that your Web browser is open and you entered the Web address for your Blackboard instance, this step shouldn't be a problem. If it is, refer to Chapter 1, and relive your first trip across the Blackboard sea.

2. **On the Course List page, click the name of your course.**

   Your course name is a hyperlink, with underlined blue text. This step takes you to a learner's view of your course.

3. **Click the Control Panel link.**

Locate this link at the bottom of the course menu on the left side of your screen. Your gut might tell you to click this link every time you want to do something important in your Blackboard course.

Managing the Course Menu

In this section of this chapter, you find instructions on how to manage the Course Menu area for the Blackboard course you're setting up. And, because learners are the reason you're utilizing the Blackboard Learning System in the first place, it makes sense to spend a little time figuring out how to make sure that they can get to what they need, when they need it.

In this section, you find out how to modify menu items on the course menu, add menu items to it, and remove menu items from it. In addition, you find out how to modify the visual design of the course menu.

To get started, go to your course Control Panel by logging in to Blackboard, clicking a course title to select it from your course list, and choosing Control Panel from the left navigation menu. All the tasks we tell you about in this section are in the Course Options pane of the Control Panel (see Figure 4-1).

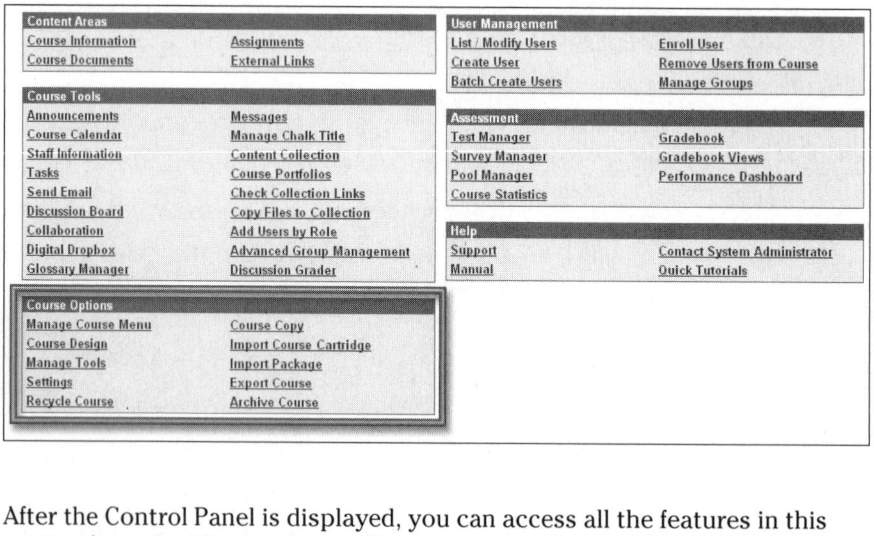

Figure 4-1:
The Course
Options
pane in the
Control
Panel.

After the Control Panel is displayed, you can access all the features in this section from the Manage Course Menu page (see Figure 4-2).

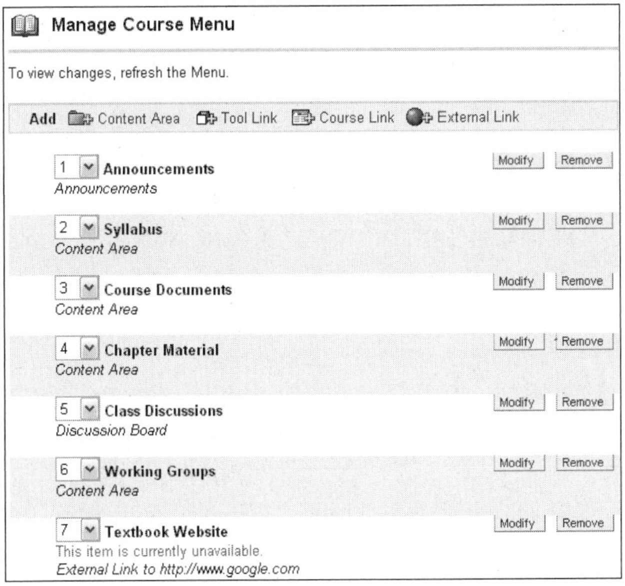

Figure 4-2:
Managing
the course
menu.

Choosing menu items

A well-organized course menu encourages learners to come to your course,
retrieve materials, do some work, and come back again, so take advantage of
the flexibility that Blackboard offers to customize your course menu. You can
modify existing menu items; remove existing items; add Content Areas, tool
links, course links, and external links; reorder the list of menu items; hide
menu items from users; and more. You get the idea. Now that you know the
possibilities, you can get started on building your course menu!

Modifying the course menu

Modifying the course menu is a key element in making the Blackboard course
your own. You can begin by changing the way buttons are labeled. Follow
these steps:

1. **Click the Modify button to the right of the menu item you want to
   change.**

   This step shows you the Update Area page, where you can select a new
   name for the area.

2. **Click the Modify button to the right of the menu item you want to
   change.**

This step shows you the Update Area page, where you can select a new name for the area.

3. **Select a name for the menu item from the Name drop-down menu (or type whatever label you like in the space immediately below this menu).**

   Keep menu item names brief (a maximum of 18 characters) if you choose to type your own.

4. **Click the Submit button (in the lower-right corner).**

   The Receipt: Success page tells you that the attempted action was successful.

5. **Click the OK button.**

   This step takes you back to the Manage Course Menu page.

If you can't see the changes you made, don't panic — refresh the menu. If you use the browser's Refresh button, you're directed to the entry page of your course, so you need to click the Control Panel link and then the Manage Course Menu link in the Course Options pane.

Kathy Munoz, Ed.D., RD, professor of exercise nutrition at Humboldt State University (California, USA) says: "To make this online learning experience fun for students and to reduce some of the fear and apprehension 'new to online learning' students may be feeling, I designed my 15-week course using a sports metaphor. Blackboard's navigation buttons are located on the left of the opening page and can be changed to reflect whatever theme you might choose to use. Some of my buttons, such as the Sports Page, I use for daily or weekly announcements; the Game Plan contains the syllabus; the Equipment Room has information related to the required textbook; and the Huddle (discussion area) is used to develop the metaphor."

Reordering the course menu

After the items on the course menu are labeled the way you prefer, you might want to change the order in which they appear. Follow these steps:

1. **Locate the menu item you want to move and click the down arrow on the drop-down menu to the left of the item (see Figure 4-3).**

   This list shows you the numbers of the menu items, with the button labeled 1 at the top.

2. **Select the number based on where you want to place the item. For example, to move your item from the fourth spot to the second (from the top), choose 2.**

The buttons immediately reorder themselves according to the new numbering structure.

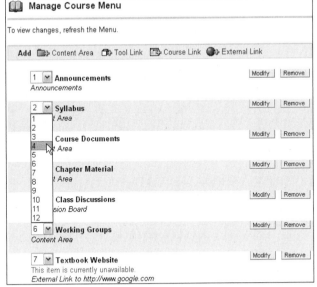

Hiding menu items

Making a menu item unavailable means that you can still see it and edit the materials in that area, but learners cannot see it in the course. Follow these steps:

1. **Locate the menu item that you want to make unavailable.**

   The item might be one you choose to reveal later in the semester or one that you simply haven't finished developing.

2. **Click the Modify button to the right of the item.**

   This step takes you to the Update Area page.

3. **Disable the Available for Student/Participant Users check box.**

   No check mark should be showing in the check box.

4. **Click the Submit button.**

   On the Success page, you see a message that the attempted action was successful.

5. **Click the OK button.**

   You're back in the Manage Course Menu area.

You made the link or button from the course menu invisible to students in the course. Unlike the Remove function (see the following section), however, the invisible item continues to be accessible from within the Control Panel for you, the instructor.

Removing menu items

Suppose that you want a permanent disappearance for a menu item and you never want to see the item again. Ever! Follow these steps:

1. **Find the unwanted menu item and click the Remove button.**

   The Remove button is to the right of the menu item's Modify button. Blackboard warns you (see Figure 4-4) that this action permanently deletes — not just hides — any item residing within this area of your course.

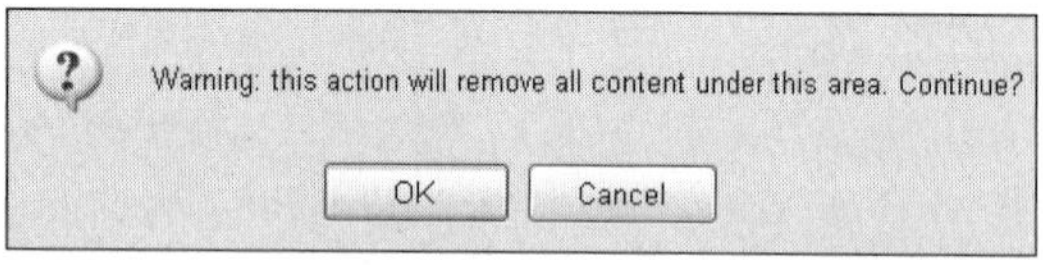

Figure 4-4:
Confirming a
deletion.

> ? Warning: this action will remove all content under this area. Continue?
>
> OK   Cancel

2. **Click the OK button if you truly want to remove the item. If not, click the Cancel button.**

   Selecting the OK button regenerates the page, and the item you selected to remove disappears. Poof! Clicking the Cancel button removes the Warning window with no effect on the course menu.

Removing a Content Area item from the course menu deletes all underlying content — you cannot retrieve the content after it's removed.

Adding menu items

Finally, it's time to add more menu items. First, however, you need to figure out what type of menu item you want to add:

- ✔ **Content area:** An empty folder where you can organize your content
- ✔ **Tool link:** Functions listed in the Course Tools area of the Control Panel that can be made available to students from the course menu
- ✔ **Course link:** An internal connection to a specific area within your Blackboard course
- ✔ **External link:** A place to reach out to the world by entering the address to a Web site outside your Blackboard course

In this set of steps, you create one of each type of menu item. To make a place for course material, follow these steps:

1. **On the Add bar atop the frame, click the Content Area option.**

   This step takes you to the Add New Area page, where you can add a new Content Area to your Blackboard course (see Figure 4-5).

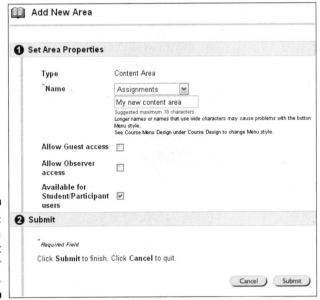

Figure 4-5:
Adding a
Content
Area in your
course.

You're adding a new area to the Content Areas pane of the Control Panel.

2. **Select a name for the button from the pull-down menu, or type one of your own choosing in the space below the drop-down menu list.**

   If you see this message:

   ```
   Action Unsuccessful, The attempted action wasn't
           successful. The label is already in use:
           Assignments. Choose another label
   ```

   it means that the name you chose for your area — in this case, Assignments — is already included on your menu list. You cannot add two Content Areas with same name.

3. **Determine who (guest, observer, or student/participant user) gets access to this area by enabling or disabling the appropriate check boxes.**

   A *guest* is a user who is given access to specific areas in a course by the instructor. An *observer,* on the other hand, is a user in the course who observes a specific student's progress in the course. By default, only the Available for Student/Participant Users selection is checked.

4. **Click the Submit button.**

   Success! You added a new Content Area to your course menu. On the Receipt: Success page, you see that your action was a success.

5. **Click the OK button.**

   This step takes you back to the Manage Course Menu page, for more fun with Blackboard.

In the next step list, you add a direct link from the menu to one of the available tools. (If you don't see the Manage Course Menu page, display it by choosing the Control Menu option from the course menu and then clicking the Manage Course Menu link in the Course Options pane.) Follow these steps:

1. **On the Add bar, click the Tool Link option.**

   The Add New Area page appears and lists the tools that are available in Blackboard at your institution (see Figure 4-6).

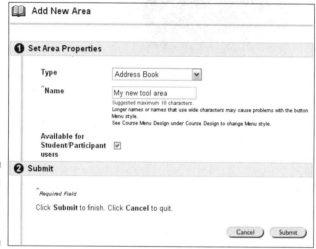

Figure 4-6:
Adding a
tool link in
your course.

2. **Click the drop-down menu to see the list of tool types.**

   This list includes tools that come with your level of Blackboard installation as well as those that your system administrator might have installed separately.

3. **Click to select the tool type you want to add to your course menu.**

   Selecting the tool type (the *function*) creates a link on the course menu so that learners can jump directly to the tool you added — for example, the Electric Blackboard.

   After you make your selection, the page regenerates and provides you with either a drop-down menu of name selections or a text field in which you type the name of the menu item, or both.

4. **Select a name or enter the name of the menu item in the Available text field.**

5. **Choose whether to make this menu item available, by enabling or disabling the check box.**

   By default, the Available check box option is checked.

6. **Click the Submit button.**

   The message on the Success: Receipt page tells you that your attempted action was successful. Another task well done!

7. **Click the OK button.**

   Guess where you are, again? That's right — you're back in the Manage Course Menu area.

How about adding a course link to the menu? Follow these steps:

1. **On the Add bar, click the Course Link option.**

   You now see the Add New Area page, where you can set the properties of the course link you're adding to the course menu (see Figure 4-7).

📖 **Add New Area**

❶ Set Area Properties

Type	Course Link
˝Name	

Suggested maximum 18 characters.
Longer names or names that use wide characters may cause problems with the button Menu style.
See Course Menu Design under Course Design to change Menu style.

Click **Browse** to choose an item.

˝Location: [Browse]

Allow Guest access ☐

Allow Observer access ☐

Available for Student/Participant users ☑

❷ Submit

˝*Required Field*

Click **Submit** to finish. Click **Cancel** to quit.

[Cancel]   [Submit]

Figure 4-7:
Adding a course link in your course.

2. **Type a name for the menu item in the Name text field.**

   Longer names or names that use wide characters can cause problems with the Menu style.

3. **Click the Browse button to locate within your Blackboard course the object (Content Area, tool, or content item, for example) to which this menu item will send students.**

   The course map appears in a separate window.

   Note that an object on the course map might have a plus sign (+) next to its folder. If you click the icon, you can drill down within the folder itself. You might need to use the scroll bar in the Course Map pop-up window to see all possible locations.

4. **Click the title of the item you want to link to.**

   The Course Map pop-up window closes after you make your selection and the path that connects to your selected item appears in the Location field on the Add New Area page.

5. **Enable or disable the check boxes to provide the desired access to this link to guests, observers, or student/participant users.**

6. **Click the Submit button.**

   On the Success: Receipt page that appears, you see a confirmation that your action was a success.

   If you forget to enter a name for the course link, the system warns you that you didn't enter a value in the Name field. You see this warning in other parts of Blackboard if you forget to enter text in a required field.

7. **Click the OK button.**

   Again, you return to the Manage Course Menu page.

To let your learners go surfing with an external link to the Web, follow these steps:

1. **From the Manage Course Menu page, click the External Link option.**

   The Add New Area page opens (see Figure 4-8).

2. **Type a name for this menu item in the Name text field.**

   This step is especially important if the Web address doesn't clearly designate what the site is about. For example, if you simply type `http://www.wafc.org`, your learners might not realize that the Web address refers to the Washington Area Frisbee Club.

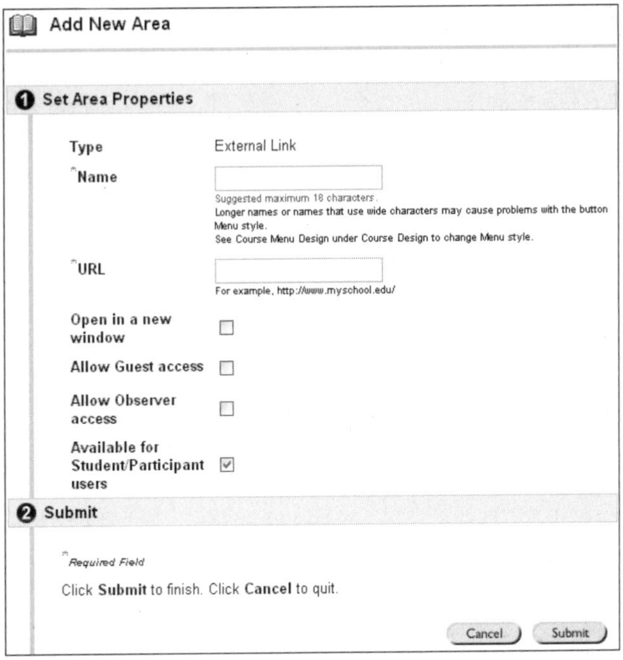

Add New Area

1 Set Area Properties

Type   External Link

"Name

    Suggested maximum 18 characters.
    Longer names or names that use wide characters may cause problems with the button
    Menu style.
    See Course Menu Design under Course Design to change Menu style.

"URL

    For example, http://www.myschool.edu/

Open in a new   ☐
window

Allow Guest access   ☐

Allow Observer   ☐
access

Available for
Student/Participant   ☑
users

2 Submit

"*Required Field*

Click **Submit** to finish. Click **Cancel** to quit.

(Cancel)   (Submit)

Figure 4-8:
Adding an
external link
in your
course.

3. Type the complete URL (Web address).

If your institution is George Washington University, for example, you
might type the address for its home page: `http://www.gwu.edu`.

Be sure to enter the URL starting with `http://`.

4. Click to enable or disable the Open in a New Window option.

Enabling this option opens another browser window when a learner
clicks the link.

Have external links (for example, an online dictionary or a currency con-
verter) open in a separate window in case learners want to refer to the
site off and on while they're using the Blackboard course.

Your students might find the preceding action confusing if their
browsers are set to block pop-ups. In addition, managing multiple open
windows can be confusing.

**5. Enable or disable the option to allow access to this menu item by
guests or observers.**

6. **Click the Submit button.**

   Once again, success! The Success: Receipt page appears.

7. **Click the OK button.**

   One more time, you're back at the Manage Course Menu page.

All new menu items appear at the bottom of the list, but you already know how to change that, right? If you want to read about how to change the order of the menu items for the first time or you simply want more practice, refer to the section "Reordering the course menu," earlier in this chapter.

Customizing the look and feel of your course menu

Customization of the look and feel of menu items on the course menu can be appealing to students and help you in gaining their attention within your Blackboard course environment. Think about your favorite Web site and ask yourself these questions:

✔ What do I like about the site?

✔ What colors does the site have?

✔ What does the color combination communicate to me?

Consider the same questions when you're creating your course menu and selecting which buttons or color combinations to use. Keep in mind one of the key design principles: KISS (Keep It Simple, Stupid)!

Okay, if you read the first half of this chapter, you labeled the menu items the way you want (and they're in the order you prefer), turned one or more items off, deleted the items you don't need, and added some new ones. What's left? Give them a makeover and change their appearance!

For these changes, return to the Control Panel and follow these steps:

1. **Click the Course Design link in the Course Options pane.**

   The Course Design page has four options: Course Menu Design, Manage Menu Display Options, Manage Tool Panel, and Course Banner.

2. **Click the Course Menu Design link.**

   The Course Menu Design page includes both the menu style selections and style properties options.

3. **Click either the Buttons or Text radio button, depending on how you want the menu items to appear on the course menu.**

   Your decision to use either the Button option or the Text option for your course menu provides you with different steps and options to configure, as described in the following subsection.

Selecting buttons

You can choose from different properties for each style, as shown in Table 4-1.

Table 4-1	Style Properties
Style	*Properties*
Button Type	Solid colors, patterns, or striped
Button Shape	Rounded corners, rounded ends, or rectangular

To select a button type, click the drop-down menu. For button shapes and button styles, click each of the radio buttons to see how the combination looks before finalizing your selections.

Click the Gallery of Buttons link to see examples of all your options. The buttons might take a second or two to appear.

Selecting text (rather than buttons)

The Style Properties section of the Course Menu Design page looks different from the way it does when you choose the buttons option. For formatting the text style on the course menu, Blackboard offers you these options:

- ✔ Background color
- ✔ Text color

Click the Pick button next to either or both of the background color or text color boxes to select the color combination for the text that appears on the buttons.

The Color Palette pops up, which allows you to choose from a variety of color options.

Even though the square color box looks like a box you're supposed to click, clicking it doesn't give you any palette options.

After you make your selection, the window closes automatically.

Be sure to have enough contrast between your background color and the text color you select. For example, stick with light text on a dark background or dark text on a light background for maximum readability.

After making your course menu design choices (either buttons or text), you have to submit your choices. Follow these steps:

1. **Click the Submit button.**

   The Success: Receipt page informs you that the settings are updated.

2. **Click the OK button.**

   You return to the Course Design options page.

To see what your new-and-improved navigation bar looks like, click the course title in the bread crumb trail of links. Looks good, right? So, what else is there to do? (If you don't know what the bread crumb trail looks like, take a peek at the one shown in Figure 1-3, over in Chapter 1.)

You need to also decide what type of display options to provide for learners in order to access the course materials: Detail view, Quick view, or both.

Detailed view provides students with the ability to drill down into the different areas of your course, much like when you're using the Course Map option in your Blackboard course. This view makes it easier to find information nested in folders.

Quick view displays only the main the titles for the different areas of your course.

By selecting both, you give students the option of choosing which view they're most comfortable with.

To select the display options for your Blackboard course, start from the Control Panel and follow these steps:

1. **Click the Course Design link in the Course Options pane.**

   You're directed to the Course Design options page.

2. **Click the Manage Menu Display Options link.**

   This step takes you to the Menu Display Options page.

3. **Click the radio button next to the display option you want your learners to have: Detail View or Quick View.**

   If you want to give them both options, click to check the box next to Allow Use of Both Views.

4. Click the Submit button.

The Success: Receipt page confirms that your action was a success.

5. Click the OK button.

You're back on the Course Design options page.

One more thing: Consider making your course more inviting and visually interesting by adding a course banner. A banner also provides an orienting element to learners while they're in the course.

You need to create this graphic outside of Blackboard by using a graphics program like Adobe Photoshop or MacPaint.

Still on the Course Design options page? If not, return to the Control Panel, click the Course Design link in the Course Options pane, and follow these steps:

1. Click the Course Banner link.

The Course Banner page appears, allowing you to upload a banner from your computer. After you put a banner in, it's displayed in the Current Banner Image box until you remove or replace it.

2. Click the Browse button.

This step opens a dialog box that allows you to navigate to the file location on your computer and choose the file. The path to the file itself is automatically inserted in the New Banner Image field.

A check box is also available on the page that allows you to remove an existing banner. Be sure to enable the box and click the Submit button.

Table 4-2 provides an overview of common Web-based image standards.

3. Click the Submit button.

The Success: Receipt page lets you know that the settings were updated.

4. Click the OK button.

You return to the Course Design options page.

Table 4-2	Web-Based Image Standards		
File Format	*When to Use It*	*When Not to Use It*	*Browser Compatibility*
GIF (Graphics Interchange Format)	When you have 256 or fewer colors and want transparency; allows high compression and animated graphics	Inadequate color representation in images with numerous colors	All
JPEG (Joint Photographic Experts Group)	For photographs that require high compression (up to 100:1); lower-quality images caused by higher compression rates; not suitable with text and straight edges	Inadequate color representation in images with numerous colors	All
PNG (Portable Network Graphics)	Alpha channel (transparency) support for both 8-bit and 24-bit color; designed to replace GIF	New and not widely supported	Limited browser (new browser) support

To see what your new course banner looks like inside your course, click the course title in the bread crumb trail of links.

The course banner appears at the top of the Announcements page. If you removed announcements from your course menu, you cannot display the banner you uploaded from the Course Banner page.

Managing the Blackboard Tools

To make good use of the tools available in Blackboard, you need to know what each one does and how it works. Don't expect your learners to know how to use all the tools just because you made them available in your course. Establish clear expectations and solid strategies when deciding to incorporate a tool — for example, Tasks — on your menu. Go as far as including in your course syllabus a section on your use of Blackboard.

Surfing the sea of tools

Blackboard offers tools within a course that help you, the instructor, communicate information to learners and set up your course content, for example.
Blackboard also has tools that you can think of as both instructor and learner
tools. For example, if you made the Send Email option visible to students
from within the Blackboard environment, both you and your learners can
send e-mail to anyone in the course (see Chapter 6). Blackboard has some
learner-only tools, such as the Homepage tool, that you, as the instructor,
cannot use. Check out Table 4-3 for a full accounting of the Blackboard tools,
sorted by user type and Blackboard version.

The Enterprise Edition of Blackboard has more tools than the Basic Edition
and allows for the addition of Building Blocks.

Table 4-3	Blackboard Tools			
Tool	*What It Does*	*Version*	*Additional Software Needed?*	*Who Uses It*
Announcements	Allows learners to view messages visible to them after they access the Announce-ments area of a course; the entry page, by default, of a Blackboard course.	All	No	Instructor
Course Calendar	Gives learners a daily, weekly, monthly, or yearly view of the duration of a course to which an instructor can post events.	All	No	Instructor
Staff Information	Provides an easy and consistent way to have contact information in a course for an instructor and other relevant personnel, like the teaching assistant or a fellow instructor.	All	No	Instructor

(continued)

Table 4-3 (continued)

Tool	What It Does	Version	Additional Software Needed?	Who Uses It
Manage Chalk Title	Provides the option of online authorization by a student before personal information is disclosed to the publisher whose resources are being accessed.	All	No	Instructor
Check Collection Links	Allows an instructor to verify the status of links to Content System items in the course.	Academic Suite only	Only if your institution has the Black-board Content System	Instructor
Copy Files to Collection	Provides a way to transfer files from a course to the Content System.	Academic Suite only	Only if your institution has the Black-board Content System	Instructor
Send Email	Enables individuals who participate in a course to send e-mail to all or selected users within the course.	All	No	Instructor, student
Messages	Facilitates the internal exchange of messages within a Blackboard course.	Academic Suite and Enterprise Edition	No	Instructor, student
Roster	Allows any course participant to view the course student roster.	All	No	Instructor
Discussion Board	Allows instructors to create discussion forums so that partici-pants in a course can post and respond to messages and thereby create threaded discussions.	All	No	Instructor, student (within a discus-sion forum)

Tool	What It Does	Version	Additional Software Needed?	Who Uses It
Digital Dropbox	Allows the exchange of files between an individual student and an instructor.	All	No	Instructor by way of the Control Panel; student
Tasks	Allow an instructor to assign to learners a prioritized list of course-related to-do's and allows learners to track the process for completing the set tasks.	All	No	Instructor, student
The Electric Blackboard	Allows learners to take notes in a course by way of an individual electronic notepad.	All	No	Instructor, student
Addressbook	Enables learners to record contact information in a course by way of an individual electronic address book.	All	No	Instructor, student
Personal Information	Permits learners to modify their personal information in the Blackboard Learning System at their institutions.	All	No	Instructor, student
Course Portfolios	Allows participants in a course to view any electronic portfolios created by using the Portfolio tool in the Blackboard Content System and shared with the course.	Academic Suite only	Only if your institution has the Blackboard Content System	Instructor

(continued)

Table 4-3 *(continued)*

Tool	What It Does	Version	Additional Software Needed?	Who Uses It
Content Collection	Provides easy access to the Blackboard Content System from the course.	Academic Suite only	Only if your institution has the Blackboard Content System	Instructor
Homepage	Offers students the option to include an electronic profile in a Blackboard course; the Homepage profile can be viewed by others in the course by using the Roster tool.	All	No	Student
My Grades	Gives students in a Blackboard course access to a summary page of their own grades in a course.	All	No	Student
Collaboration	Allows for real-time interaction in a Blackboard course.	All	Java plug-in	Instructor, student
Glossary Manager	Offers a way to create and view the glossary of terms for a course.	All	No	Instructor

Opting in or out of Blackboard tools

How do you decide which tools to use? How do you decide which tools to turn off for use by your learners? Is there any method to this madness? Yes! Opting in or out of Blackboard depends on how you're planning to use the Blackboard environment to meet your instructional goals and those of your students.

Review Table 4-1 to determine which tools you want to use in your course. You can add these tools in two ways from the Manage Tools page. From the Control Panel, follow these steps:

1. **Click the Manage Tools link in the Course Options pane.**

   You're now on the Manage Tools page. Three options are on this page: Tool Availability, Building Block Availability, and Content Type Availability. In the first set of steps in this section, we walk you through the use of the Tool Availability options.

2. **Click the Tool Availability link (see Figure 4-9).**

   You now see a screen with a four-column table with the column headings Tool, Available, Allow Guest, and Allow Observer. Under the Allow Guest and Allow Observer columns are some grayed-out circles. They simply indicate that a particular tool isn't applicable for that column.

   Enabling and disabling the check boxes in the three rightmost columns is what we describe in this section.

   If you don't see one of these tools listed as an option, it might be turned off at the system administrator level. Check with that person to determine which ones are turned off.

Figure 4-9:
Tool
Availability
options.

Tool	Available	Allow Guest	Allow Observer
External tools from Pearson Education External tools from Pearson Education	☑	●	●
Address Book Address Book	☑	●	☐
Announcements Announcements	☑	☑	☑
Adaptive Release Adaptive Release	☑	●	●
Glossary Glossary	☑	●	●
Copy Files to Collection Copy Files to Collection	☑	●	●
Check Collection Links Check Collection Links	☑	●	●

Tool Availability

Some institutions don't allow guest or observer access to courses (refer to the section "Adding menu items," earlier in this chapter). Check with your Blackboard administrator to find out your institution's policy for guest and observer access.

To make a tool available in the course, simply check the box in the Available column for the tool you want to use or want your learners to use.

To make a tool unavailable, uncheck the box or click inside the checked box in the Available column. This action removes the check mark.

3. Enable the tools you want to use and disable those you don't.

The number of tools displayed on this page varies with the type of Blackboard Learning System license your institution has: Enterprise or Basic. Be sure to check with your institution's Blackboard system administrator for more details regarding your institution's license.

4. Click the Submit button.

The Success: Receipt page for Tool Availability displays a confirmation of your successful action.

5. Click the OK button.

This step takes you to the Manage Tools page, with the three options Tool Availability, Building Block Tool Availability, and Content Type Availability displayed.

6. Click the Building Block Tool Availability link.

You're now on the Building Block Tool Availability page.

Building Blocks are third-party components that can be added to the Blackboard Learning System to provide additional enhancements to the Blackboard environment, such as Discussion Grader, MERLOT Library Search, Copyright Management, and Advanced Group Management. Many Building Blocks are listed on the Blackboard Web site (www.blackboard.com). Your organization or institution might have installed third-party Building Blocks or developed some in-house. To obtain more information, check with your institution's Blackboard system administrator (the best friend who keeps on giving).

Building Blocks are available only in the Learning System *Enterprise* Edition. If you don't see an active link to select, you're using the *Basic* version and don't have access to this area. If you see the Building Block Tool Availability link, you're using the *Enterprise* version. The list of available Building Blocks that's displayed varies because the blocks must be downloaded and installed by your Blackboard system administrator.

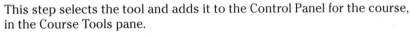

7. **Enable the Available check box.**

   This step selects the tool and adds it to the Control Panel for the course, in the Course Tools pane.

   To make a Building Block unavailable in the course, simply click the checked box and the check mark disappears.

8. **Click the Submit button.**

   You see the Success: Receipt page for the Building Block Tool Availability option.

9. **Click the OK button.**

   The Manage Tools page is displayed.

In Blackboard, you can make certain tools available on your list of tool options in Content Areas. The following set of steps shows you how to make content tools available by using Content Tool Availability. From the Control Panel, follow these steps:

1. **Click the Manage Tools link in the Course Options pane.**

2. **Click the Content Type Availability link.**

   The Content Type Availability page lists the various content items you can make available or unavailable in the Content Areas.

3. **Enable the Available check box to select a content type.**

   To make a content type unavailable in the course, simply disable the check box and the check mark disappears.

4. **Click the Submit button.**

   The Success: Receipt is displayed for the changes you made in the Content Type Availability area.

5. **Click OK to return to the Manage Tools page.**

6. **Click OK again.**

You should see the course Control Panel. Does your Course Tools pane look different? To see your changes, select the course name from the bread crumb links and select the Course Tools link from the course menu.

Choosing what the learner gets

If you know what tools are available and how to use them in your Blackboard course, you should decide what your learners get to see (refer to the section "Surfing the sea of tools," earlier in this chapter, for a description). The steps in this section show you a simple way to make tools available or unavailable to your students.

Just because you turn on a tool for your students doesn't mean that they get to see it! Remember to go back to the Manage Course Menu page to add a tool and create a menu button for your learners to access it.

From the course menu, choose the Control Panel option and follow these steps:

1. **Click the Manage Course Menu link in the Course Options pane.**

2. **Click the Add Tool option.**

   The Add New Area page is displayed.

3. **Click the drop-down menu and select Tools Area.**

   The page regenerates and `Tools` is displayed in the Name text field. If you want to change the name of the tool, type it in the text box.

   If the Available for Student/Participant Users check box isn't checked, click inside the check box to make the area available to your learners.

4. **Click the Submit button.**

   The Success: Receipt page is displayed.

5. **Click OK to go back to the Manage Course Menu page.**

   This step takes you back to the Manage Course Menu page.

6. **Click the Modify button for the Tools area you just added.**

   If you want to make a tool unavailable, click the Unavailable radio button. This action removes the tool from the learner's view in the Blackboard course.

7. **Click the Submit button.**

   The Success: Receipt page confirms that your action was a success.

8. **Click the name of your course in the bread crumb link trail atop the white frame.**

   This step takes you to the entry page of the course: Display view.

9. **Click the Tool area menu item you just added to the course menu.**

   This step takes you to the Tools page you enabled for your learners.

As the instructor of the course, you cannot access the Digital Dropbox, Homepage, and My Grades tools from the Tools page.

Chapter 5

Building Your Class Materials

In This Chapter

▶ Putting content into a Content Area

▶ Using the Item options

▶ Modifying content

▶ Editing from Display view

▶ Organizing content

▶ Determining content availability

*A*fter you have learners in your course and have customized its look and feel, it's time to put class materials where it counts. In this chapter, you discover the magic behind posting information to Blackboard and the best ways to keep the information in order, and when to make it accessible to your learners. This chapter is a biggie — in both length and importance! Have fun! Be careful!

For all the features described in this chapter, you should start at your course Control Panel. That's right: Begin at your Blackboard headquarters, by following these steps:

1. **Log in to Blackboard by using your username and password.**

   Assuming that you opened your Web browser and entered the Web address for your Blackboard instance, this step shouldn't be a problem. If it is, check out Chapter 15 and then talk to your best friend, your Blackboard system administrator.

2. **On your Course List page, click the name of your course.**

   Your course name is a hyperlink, underlined and in blue text. This step lets you see the way learners see your course.

3. **Click the Control Panel link.**

   The link is at the bottom of the course menu, on the left side of your screen. (Click this link every time you want to do something important in your Blackboard course.)

Even though we think that you should do everything as an instructor from the course Control Panel, for consistency's sake, you can save one click to add or edit course materials in any Content Area, by using *Edit view*. After you log in to Blackboard and click your course, look for the Edit View link, in the upper-right corner of the white frame. Whenever you click this link, you see a page from which you can use the Add bar to add materials, and you still see the course menu to the left.

Just because we tell you about Edit view, don't convince yourself that it works for every single task in Blackboard. You use it just in Content Areas, and we still think that you should do everything through the Control Panel. It's your single point for success.

Managing Content in a Content Area

Remember the days when you had to carry a huge stack of syllabi to your first class, and then the next week you had to carry a 4-foot stack of readings? No more. Upload away! In this section, we tell you how to create content directly in your Blackboard course, by using the Visual Text Box Editor to upload files from your computer into your Blackboard course and to organize, modify, and remove content.

Creating content in the Visual Text Box Editor

The Visual Text Box Editor, shown in Figure 5-1, provides a place to type text directly or paste text copied from another application, like Microsoft Word. When you use the Visual Text Box Editor, you literally create text to appear on the Web page within your course. It's the same as writing your own online newspaper, but different.

Figure 5-2 shows you a zoomed-in picture of the three rows of tools that are part of the Visual Text Box Editor. (The figure is also shown on the Cheat Sheet inside the front cover of this book.)

In Internet Explorer Version 5.5 and higher in Windows, the Visual Text Box Editor has multiple rows of editing tools, for applying bold, italics, and color. All other browser programs — like Netscape, Firefox, and Safari — have only a basic text-entry area.

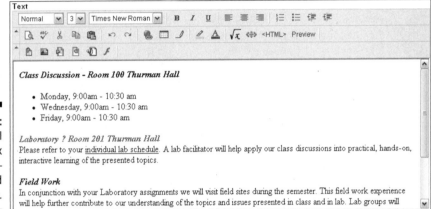

Figure 5-1:
The Visual
Text Box
Editor —
form and
function.

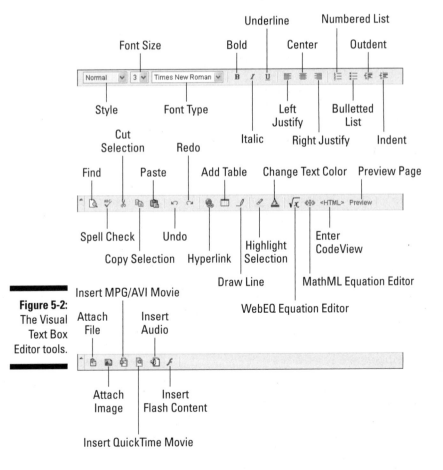

Figure 5-2:
The Visual
Text Box
Editor tools.

Elizabeth Sanchez, a high school poetry teacher at Virtual High School, says: "When it comes to what my learners 'hear,' format is everything. A little bit of formatting does much to make me 'sound like me' online. It's how I convey my caring yet firm personality to my online learners. I have butterflies for every week, and they are color coordinated with the bars and buttons; there are tables and bulleted lists galore. Friendly yet organized is the tone [that's] conveyed."

To create some content in the Visual Text Box Editor, follow these steps:

1. **Starting from the Control Panel, click any Content Area link in the Content Areas pane.**

   Your institution probably has some default Content Areas already available for you to use. If not, for information on creating a Content Area, refer to the section in Chapter 4 about adding menu items.

2. **On the next page, click the Item option to add a Content Item.**

   This step brings up a screen with four sections: Content Information, Content, Options, and Submit.

3. **In the first section, enter a name for the Content Item you're adding.**

   Be consistent when you name items. For example, if you refer to your notes as *lecture notes* in the syllabus, call them that in your Blackboard course too.

4. **If you want, choose a color for the name you just entered by clicking the Pick button.**

   A color palette pops up in a new window for your color choice.

5. **Select a color for the item name by picking the color you want from the palette that's displayed.**

   Although Blackboard provides a wide range of hues to select from, keep in mind that lighter shades might be difficult to read on the white screen background. For example, select dark red so that you see plenty of contrast.

6. **Place the cursor by clicking in the large text box.**

   You might need to scroll down to see the text box.

   Notice along the top of the text box some buttons that function like word processor functions — such as Bold, Italics, and Underline — in addition to a font menu, alignment icons, and bulleted list features. (See the Cheat Sheet, too.)

7. **Enter some text in the text box.**

   As with a word processing program, you can also paste text from another document into this text field.

When you copy or paste from another program, like Microsoft Word, the text might lose some formatting.

8. **When you finish typing your text, skip past Section 2 – Content and go directly to Section 3 – Options. Again, you might need to scroll down to see Section 3.**

   Section 3 is described in the following subsection.

9. **Select Yes or No for the Make Content Available option.**

   Selecting Yes makes this text available to learners as soon as you click the Submit button. If you select No, learners don't have access to the text until you return later and select Yes.

10. **Select Yes or No for the Track Number of Views option.**

    The Tracking feature is a useful way to determine which, if any, learners have opened this item. For more information, look in the Chapter 9 section about tracking views.

11. **Choose the Date and Time Restrictions option, if you want.**

    This optional step allows you to make the item available or unavailable on a specific date and time.

    - To have this item automatically become *available* on a specific date and time, enable the Display After check box and make the appropriate selections from the drop-down menus for month, date, year, and time.

    - To have this item automatically become *unavailable* on a specific date and time, enable the Display Until check box and make the appropriate selections from the drop-down menus for month, date, year, and time.

    - For either of these options, you can click the calendar icon to see a pop-up calendar from which you can select the date.

12. **Click the Submit button.**

    The next page displays the Success heading to confirm your activity. Click OK to return to the Content Area.

To look at the content you just added from the perspective of your learners, click the course title link in the bread crumb trail of links.

Adding content created elsewhere

In many cases, you want to create content by using software other than Blackboard — a word processor or spreadsheet package, for example. In this section, we give you directions for adding to your Blackboard course some content that you've already saved on your computer or other storage device.

As always, start from the Control Panel. (If it's not already displayed, choose the Control Panel option from the course menu to get there.) This step list is long, but effective:

1. **Click any Content Area link.**

   If no Content Area in your Blackboard course meets your needs, refer to the section in Chapter 4 about adding menu items for instructions on how to add Content Areas.

2. **Click the Item option on the next page.**

   The next screen that's displayed has four sections: Content Information, Content, Options, and Submit.

3. **Enter a name for this item in the first section.**

   Make sure that you choose a name that learners can distinguish from other items you might add later. Naming the item Notes1 is okay, but it's not nearly as descriptive as Cell Mitosis Notes.

4. **Click the Pick button to select a color for the item name you just entered, if you want.**

   This step is optional, but it might be helpful to your learners to color-code items by unit, for example.

5. **Click to select a color for the item name from the palette.**

   Keep in mind that lighter shades are difficult to read on the screen's white background.

6. **In the large text box, enter any information you want to provide in addition to the document you will add.**

   This information can include a brief description of the item you're adding, a due-date reminder, or other information.

7. **In Section 2, click the Browse button to the right of the Attach Local File option.**

   This button enables you to search your computer for the file you want to add to your site.

   To upload a file directly in the text box and therefore integrate it seamlessly into the text description, click the Attach File button (the paper-with-paper-clip icon) on the third row of buttons in the Visual Text Editor (see the Cheat Sheet inside the front cover).

8. **Locate the file on your computer, and then click the filename and click the Open button.**

   Figure 5-3 shows you what you might see on your computer when you browse to find your file. The filename appears in the field directly to the left of the Browse button.

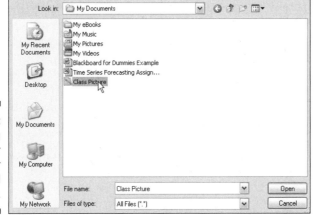

Figure 5-3:
Browsing
your
computer
to find and
upload files.

9. **If your institution uses the Blackboard Content System, you can click the Browse button to the right of the Link to Content Collection Item option.**

   A window pops up from which you can select your previously stored file and click the Submit button.

10. **In the Name of Link to File field, you type the *hyperlink* that learners click in order to view the item you're adding.**

    If you leave this field blank, Blackboard enters the filename (for example, lecturenotesunit4.doc) instead.

11. **For the next step, choose one of the three options from the drop-down menu:**

    • **Create a Link to This File:** You select this option for most items you add to your course. This action makes a link that learners click to view the file. You use this default setting most of the time when you add content to your Blackboard course.

    • **Display Media File within the Page:** This option embeds media files (photos, graphs, and charts, for example) directly on the page instead of creating a link to the file. *Note:* If you select this option, you don't need to enter text for the Name of Link to This File field in Step 10 because there's no need for a link.

    • **Unpackage This File:** Choose this option when the file you're adding has been zipped (compressed) with software designed for that purpose.

12. **In Section 3 – Options, click the Yes or No radio button to set the availability of the item.**

    Choosing Yes makes the item available immediately after clicking the Submit button. Choosing No makes the item unavailable to your learners until you return and click the Yes button later.

13. **Next, click the Yes or No radio button for the Track Number of Views option.**

    Enabling item tracking (that is, choosing Yes) allows you to find out how many learners, if any, have viewed the item. For more information on using the Tracking feature, see the section in Chapter 9 about tracking views.

14. **Enable the Display After check box and the Display Until check box if you want to choose date and time restrictions.**

    This optional step allows you to make the item available or unavailable on a specific date and time. The following list describes how to make a Content Item available or unavailable:

    • To have this item automatically become *available* on a specific date and time, enable the Display After check box and make the appropriate selections from the pull-down menus for month, date, year, and time.

    • To have this item automatically become *unavailable* on a specific date and time, enable the Display Until check box and make the appropriate selections from the pull-down menus for month, date, year, and time.

    • For either of these options, you can click the calendar icon to see a pop-up calendar from which you can select the date.

15. **Click the Submit button.**

    The receipt page labeled Success confirms that you've added new content to your site. Click OK to return to the Content Area.

To look at the content you just added from the perspective of your learners, click the course title link in the bread crumb trail of links.

Editing with ease by using the Display view and Edit view

At the beginning of this chapter, we tip you off to the easiest and fastest way to manage your content in any Content Area in your Blackboard course. And we're telling the truth! Blackboard has a toggle switch (the Edit View link) that acts much like an on–off switch.

Clicking the Edit View link from your learners' view of the course lets you into the editing view of a Content Area, where you can add, modify, manage, and remove content. After you finish editing your Content Area, you can use the Display View toggle link to return to your learners' view to check your edits. The process is smooth! Figure 5-4 lets you compare Display view and Edit view of a Content Area in a Blackboard course.

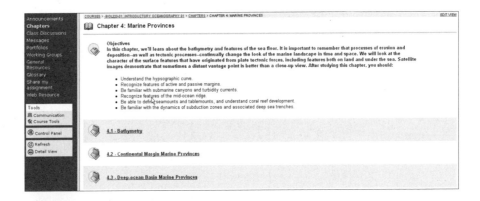

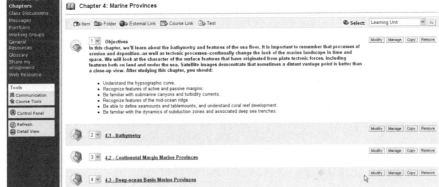

Figure 5-4:
From learner's view (Display view) to Edit view.

You can see the Edit View link in the upper-right corner of a Content Area page whenever you browse your Blackboard course from the learner or display view. The toggle link is named Display View.

To edit or add content to any of the Content Areas in your Blackboard course, follow these steps:

1. **From the learner's view of the course (the entry page), click a Content Area link or button on your course menu.**

   In the right frame of your Blackboard window, you see either the Content Area items you added or, if you're starting from scratch, a Folder Empty note.

   Blackboard refers to Content Areas as *folders*. Content Areas are the top-level folders in your Blackboard course. Within a Content Area or folder, you can create subfolders.

2. **Click the Edit View link in the upper-right corner of your Content Area page.**

Your view changes to display the available editing tools in the Content Area, such as the Item, Folder, and External Link options.

3. Use the available tools to add or edit content in the Content Area.

This chapter focuses on how you can add or edit content in the Content Areas of your Blackboard course.

4. After you finish your edits or additions to your content in the Content Area, click the Display View link.

You're back in Display (learner) view of your Blackboard course. Review your content from this view so that you experience what your learners do whenever they navigate your course.

Adding World Wide Web links

Sometimes it makes sense to use materials that are available on the Web to support, enhance, and supplement your Blackboard content. Adding a Web link to a Content Area offers a potentially great payoff with little extra effort. Follow these steps:

1. From the Control Panel (from the course menu, select the Control Panel option), click any Content Area link in the Content Areas pane.

Although you might already have a Content Area available and named External Links (or something similar), you can put links in any Content Area.

2. Click External Link to add a link to this Content Area.

The page that appears has four sections: External Link Information, Content, Options, and Submit.

3. Type a name for the link in the Name field (see Figure 5-5).

Because learners don't see the URL, the name should indicate where the link will take them.

4. Enter the URL (the Web address) in the URL field.

Be sure to include the entire address here (yes, even all the http:// characters at the beginning). Don't worry if you forget to add the address: Blackboard alerts you that you're missing the http:// information.

5. A text box is provided so that you can add explanatory material, if you want.

Although this step is optional, consider adding a brief statement describing the site that's being linked to, or how it's relevant to the course content.